John of the Cross

THE WAY OF THE CHRISTIAN MYSTICS

GENERAL EDITOR

Noel Dermot O'Donoghue, ODC

Volume 10

John of the Cross

by

Ross Collings, O.C.D.

A Michael Glazier Book
THE LITURGICAL PRESS
Collegeville, Minnesota

About the Author

Ross Collings is presently Prior and Student-Master at the house of studies of the Australian region of the Discalced Carmelites in Melbourne; he teaches Systematic Theology at the Yarra Theological Union, Box Hill. After graduating in Arts at the University of Adelaide, he completed philosophical and theological studies at the Milltown Institute, Dublin, and was awarded D. Phil. in theology at Oxford in 1978 with a thesis on Aquinas and John of the Cross.

Typography by Phyllis Boyd LeVane.

1   2   3   4   5   6   7   8   9

Library of Congress Cataloging-in-Publication Data
Collings, Ross.
      John of the Cross / by Ross Collings.
            p.   cm. — (The Way of the Christian mystics ; v. 10)
      Includes bibliographical references.
      ISBN 0-8146--5627-7
      1. John of the Cross, Saint, 1542-1591. 2. Mysticism—Spain-
-History—16th century. 3. Mysticism—Catholic Church. 4. Catholic
Church—Doctrines—History—16th century. I. Series.
BX4700.J7C59   1990
248.2'2'092—dc20   90-62038
                                                                              CIP

Contents

Editor's Preface

Up to quite recently mystics were either misunderstood or simply not understood. But now we are coming to see that, in T.S. Eliot's words, the way of the mystics is "our only hope, or else despair." As the darkness deepens, and the lights go out, those ancient lights begin to appear and to show us the way forward. They are not only lights to guide us, but are each a human countenance in which we can recognise something of ourselves—each is a portrait for self-recognition.

Unfortunately, the great Christian mystics have been generally presented as models of perfection or monuments of orthodoxy—sometimes, too, as inhumanly joyless and ascetical. Yet they were, above all else, men and women of feeling, always vulnerable, at times perhaps insecure and uncertain of the way ahead. For all that, they all shine with a special divine likeness and a special human radiance.

Each of the following portraits tries to present a true likeness of its subject, a likeness that comes alive especially in the ordinary and the everyday. In each case the author has been asked to enliven scholarship with personal warmth, and to temper enthusiasm with accurate scholarship. Each portrait hopes to be in its own way a work of art, something carefully and lovingly fashioned out of genuine material.

The main focus nevertheless is on the way in which each mystic mediates the Christian Gospel, and so gives us a deeper, richer, clearer vision of the Christian mystery. This kind of exposition demands the reader's full and prayerful attention. Each book is the story of a pilgrimage, for the mystic, the writer and the reader.

Noel O'Donoghue

1

Introduction

The West front of Avila cathedral could stand as an emblem of the immense cultural and spiritual vitality of Castile—and of one of her greatest sons, Juan de Yepes/St. John of the Cross. A clear plane of perfectly dressed hard stone, lean and austere, it presents a face of sheer, pure durability. There is a suggestion almost of military rigour about it; indeed, the further end of the same cathedral, the apse or holy of holies, itself forms part of the city walls which defied the Moorish armies. But set in the midst of this pristine facade, the mediaeval doorway and the baroque screen over the west window are sculpted with an intense sensuous energy, as though all the resources of animation have been drawn from the surrounding surface to be concentrated in this small framework of convoluted stone. Through this door one has access to the inner holy place where Christ dwells. The result of this juxtaposing of austerity and opulence is quite startling. And yet there is no discordance; the integrity of the whole, both in Cathedral facade and Castilian genius, lies not in the reconciling but in the containing of fierce opposites. The vibrant tension between them is more truly characteristic of this Spanish world than is any one of the elements taken in isolation.

What does this emblem signify concerning St. John? It could be read in many features of the man. "Though small in stature [scarcely five feet tall], I believe he is great in God's eyes", as his Carmelite sister and soul-friend Teresa of Jesus affectionately observed.[1] His religious life was always manifestly austere, capable at times of disconcerting not only the comfortable piety of devout gentry, but even the wise, vigorous asceticism of Teresa;[2] and yet there was nothing of him that was harsh or tense, but he bore a compelling aura of humane, gentle, unaffected serenity—*alegre, amable, sereno* recur constantly in descriptions of his face and presence. The habitual frugality he required of himself and of the communities he governed exploded at times in extravagant gestures of kindness in food and medicine for the poor and the sick. He nursed these sick himself with an exquisite care that seemed feminine in its tenderness, their humiliation of physical wretchedness giving way entirely to an experience of simple immediate affection; yet there was hardly another man in Spain so strong-minded and unsentimental—standing unmoved in a matter of practical affairs against the usually all-conquering feminine charm of Teresa[3] and, in a matter of principle, against nine months' brutal imprisonment and brow-beating from his brethren in Toledo. There was about him an innate reserve; but in conversation with him many experienced themselves to be sympathetically understood in a unique and astounding depth— he met and engaged them in regions where they had not known themselves before.[4] His constant turning to places of solitude did not inhibit easy companionship with the brethren. The love of seclusion, inherited in a living tradition from the hermits of Mount Carmel, coexisted in him with a zeal which drove him to bring gospel and sacrament to the poor isolated villages around Duruelo.

John's character is thus marked by rich and vigorous cross-currents. In meeting him, however, people found—or, in the communion of saints, we can still find—a person of unerring integrity and wholeness: no hint of prevarication or inconsistency here. Indeed, one could speak of him as "paradoxical"

---

[1] *Letters,* X, ed. E. Allison Peers, London, 1951. Vol I, p 52.

[2] *Foundations,* ch. 14.

[3] *Letters, loc. cit.*

[4] c.f. Testimony of M. Magdalen of the Holy Spirit, *Complete Works of St. John of the Cross,* trans. and ed. E. Allison Peers, 1974, p 297

only by observing him from a distance and noting the attributes in a remote and uincomprehending way. Really to meet him in a living encounter reveals a sheer rightness and harmony of all that he is—truly *monachos,* the solitary single-hearted and unified man in whom the centre of personal existence is so truly realized that it holds together powerfully and sweetly all these diverse energies of character.

But if now we ask just what is that central unifying factor of his person, we find a still deeper mystery which eludes any simple psychological analysis. The "central point" of the man is not a focus to be grasped or held in place, but a certain dynamism or self-transcending which of its nature cannot be arrested. This mysterious quality is indeed true of every person created in the image of God who cannot be grasped. It is especially true of a saint, in whom there is restored the original holiness of the divine image. However, St. John of the Cross seems to have a particular charism of vividly manifesting that general human and Christian truth. There is a certain elusive quality about him which is very marked, all the more so since it seems to stand in contrast with the strong, distinct colours of his character. Far from being dispelled by familiarity with him, it is as though the more closely one approaches him, the more one finds that his centre lies elsewhere, because it is given away, is transparent to another. We cannot simply lay hold of him.

If, then, we propose to trace "the way of St.. John of the Cross" and so come to understand him more closely, we must at the outset be alerted to the enigmatic nature of that way:

> In order to arrive at what you are not, you must go by a way where you are not.[5]

John of the Cross himself fulfilled that precept eminently. And what, for him, is that Way? Only Jesus Christ. And so, everything that we discern about John—his doctrine, his aesthetic gifts, his character—all must be understood as continuously surrendered to the one who surrendered Himself for him.

[5] *Asc,* I, 13, 11.

Indeed, perhaps we would do better to translate his precept not as "In order to *arrive (Para venir a)*. . .", but more literally as "to *come to*. . ."; his Christian existence even in its perfection is best understood not as a point of arrival, not as an enclosed, ultimately autonomous self, but as a continuous act of turning from self to the Beloved, a coming towards the one who has called him. This man who had such a powerful air of tranquil self-possession was so precisely because inwardly he was wholly dispossessed of self. The "foolishness" of that statement is the foolishness of the gospel and of St. John's vowed life—"of the Cross":

> I have been crucified with Christ; it is no longer I who live, but Christ who lives in me; and the life I now live in the flesh I live by faith in the Son of God, who loved me and gave himself for me.
>
> (Gal 2:20)

It must not be thought that this spiritual selflessness diminishes or obliterates the particular psychological features of the believer, nor the innermost reality of his person. Quite the opposite: these are made all the more pure and clear and strong to the extent that he surrenders himself in love to God. While it is Christ who lives here, it is still John who lives—Christ, as it were, with the lineaments of John, unique, un-·mistakably this one and no other, yet being so because entirely turned away from self into the life of Christ through having received Christ's own gift of himself.

We shall trace this way of St. John through his writings. That might seem quite unexceptional and inevitable, and indeed it is the only way available. But in fact it is a very bold thing to attempt and requires a particular quality of reading without which the central purpose of his work is rendered futile. That quality is the communion of living—of loving—faith. Or, one might say, of prayer, taken in its broad and profound sense of experiencing oneself to be in need, in need of God's grace and opened to it. We must heed what John himself says about this in the Prologue to his commentary on the *Spiritual Canticle*.[6] Firstly, he declares at the beginning of this prose commentary that the more adequate expression of what he has to say will always be the poem itself. Morever, "these stanzas have been composed from within a love which comes from an abounding mystical understanding" (*Cant, Prol,* 2): the language is that of a lover, treasured and eloquent to those involved, but likely to be inane to the bystander. The imaginative language, John says, spills over the calculated limits of rational prose, welling up from a fertile experience of love which of its nature will always retain the quality of wonder, of "secret mysteries" (*loc. cit* 1), and which is therefore best expressed in forms which are "strange" (*extrañas*) to the grasp of common discourse. And yet the source of this energetic profusion of language is the immediacy of loving encounter with God, which is itself sheer and simple. Consequently, as the expression of such a reality, the poetry must be heard with something of that same simplicity of spirit (*Ibid*). It is the language of the Gospel "infants", not of the learned and clever. In presenting his text in this way, John invites us to meet him in that same region of simple loving encounter with Christ, the mutual recognition of friends in a common ultimate Friend. Anything less than that shared faith might deliver a rich store of ideas and aesthetic experience; but the person himself, and the heart of his teaching and experience, is to be found only in the communion of saints, no matter how indigent our own place in it might be.

If the marks of authentic friendship are freedom, respect and trust, then the way of St. John of the Cross offers these things—and requires them—to a remarkable degree. In what amounts to an apology for presenting one specific interpretation of the poem in his commentary, he observes that "it is better to leave the sayings of love in their fullness, so that each person might draw advantage from them according to his own way and measure of spirit, rather than limiting them to one meaning to which not every taste (*paladar*) can fit itself" (*loc cit,* 2). That might seem to be a recipe for wholesale sub-

---

[6]Addressed to Mother Anne of Jesus, Prioress of the Carmelite convent of Granada.

jectivism and arbitrariness of interpretation, eroding the possibility of any real shared meaning; and so it would be, if the spirit of the poetry were merely human and individualistic. But in fact it is quite otherwise. It is "the Spirit of the Lord, who helps us in our weaknesses" (*loc cit*, 1; Rom 8:26), who is the unifying power of this communion of faith by inspiring both speaker and hearer. John happily renounces all personal dogmatizing even on his own poetry, not because he abdicates responsibility for the truth, but because the truth of his poetry, and especially the existential "truth" of his reader's experience of it, is ultimately in Christ's hands, not his. Christ is the way, and the Spirit of Christ is the living guide. Such a profound respect for spiritual freedom might seem to be an unlikely quality in a classic work of the Spanish Counter-Reformation. Nevertheless, it is entirely consistent with the mystical genesis of John's experience and writing. His own perception of God is utterly *given* to him—in the word of the Scriptures proclaimed by the Church (*loc. cit,* 4; *Asc,* Prol, 2) and in the Spirit enabling him to hear that word; therefore we will always find him, as a true teacher of these mysteries, giving way to that primacy of God.

Thus Mother Anne of Jesus, at whose request the *Canticle* commentary was written, might lack familiarity with scholastic theology, but nevertheless

> you do not lack that mystical theology, which is known through love, in which [divine truths] are not only known but also experienced.[7]

John is here consciously echoing one of the great primary text of the Christian mystical tradition, from *The Divine Names* of Dionysius the Areopagite, a pseudonymous writer, probably Syrian, of the fifth century. Speaking of his teacher Hierotheus, Dionysius regards his wisdom as flowing from the diligent study of Scripture and tradition and also from "that more mysterious inspiration, not only learning but also experiencing

---

[7]"...no solamente se saben, mas juntamente se gustan" (*Cant,* Prol, 4).

the divine things".[8] John translates this notion of "experiencing" the things of God with a word (*se gustan*) which emphasizes the immediacy and the non-conceptual quality of this perception, something which pertains to the "spiritual senses" or the "taste" for God. But the whole context shows that he has not lost the original Greek sense of "undergoing" (*pathōn*), "suffering", "being passive to" the intervention of God. Mother Anne will recognise in his writings not so much a common talent or achievement, but rather the same energizing and illuminating intervention from a transcendent Giver.

What St. John is offering us, then, is not an abstract theological insight, but a recognition of actual Christian experience. His whole work, poetry and prose, is an existential theology, immediately personal and experiential. For all the rich imagery and powerful symbols at work in his writing, the drama of redemption and sanctification unfolds in the concrete lives of entirely real persons—on the one hand, Christ the Beloved, the Spouse, and on the other, the Bride, "the soul" (*el alma*). Modern readers are liable to have a particular difficulty with "the soul". There is the suspicion that it indicates a genre of mere allegory, of pious fantasy removed from the real life of actual people; or, even worse, that it betrays a Platonist misconception of the human person, as though only the non-material, spiritual dimension were ultimately of any value. The true identity of the soul in St. John, is quite different. It is a "biographical" subject, (or, even better, autobiographical), viewed in the actuality of Christian experience. Most often it means not the generalized, formal concept of "the human person", nor even "the Christian person", but simply "I".

It would seem that John has two reasons for using this traditional term rather than speaking overtly in the first person. Firstly, inasmuch as "the soul" is indeed himself and the experience described is his own, it is nevertheless not himself as an independent, heroic protagonist of a spiritual adventure, but himself always and only in relationship to Christ. "I" can pretend to stand solitary, but the Bride-soul is always identified

---

[8]"...ou monon mathōn alla kāi pathōn ta theia" (*Div.N.* II, 648 B) c.f. *Pseudo-Dionysius. The Complete Works*, trans. Colm Luibheid, London, 1987, p 65.

by her relationship to Christ the Spouse. There could be no greater irrelevance for John than to regale his readers with an intimate, confiding account of his spiritual life with himself at the centre. He knows that the authenticity and enduring value of his person and experience lies in his being given over to Christ, and that this gift of self is effected through being assumed into the universal Person of the Church-Bride.

> And so that what I say (which I desire to submit to better judgment, and totally to that of Holy Mother Church) might be better accepted, I do not mean to affirm anything that is mine, trusting myself to my own experience or to that of any other spiritual persons ... (although I intend to make use of both), unless it is confirmed and expounded by authorities from divine Scripture.
>
> (*Cant*, Prol, 4)

In an age which saw the emergence of an intense individualism in European culture, this is striking testimony to the abiding power of the Catholic sense of the community of faith expressed in a living tradition. *El alma* of the *Ascent / Dark Night,* of the *Spiritual Canticle* and the *Living Flame* is *anima ecclesiastica,* John himself bearing the form of the Church, having become perfectly realized in his identity by entrusting (*fiandome*) everything about himself into her creative, sustaining word of Revelation.

The writing is in fact intensely personal, to a degree measured by the enormous love that inspired it. But the subjective quality has been entirely purified, ordered and transformed in the subjectivity of God:

> Oh night which guided me!
> Oh night more lovely than the dawn!
> Oh night which joined
> Beloved with lover,
> Lover transformed in the Beloved!
>
> (*D.N.* st. 5)

In order to get some notion of just how personal is his commentary concerning the soul, we have to take to heart—as far as each one's own poor heart can do—the sheer free, happy, tender, uninhibited love-making of the Bride's song, recognizing the intensity of poetic Eros to be the Agape of John's union with Christ.

> Upon my flowering breast,
> Kept wholly for himself alone,
> There he stayed sleeping,
> And I caressed him
> And the fanning of the cedars made a breeze.
>
> The breeze was from the turret;
> When I parted his locks,
> With his gentle hand
> He wounded my neck
> And all my senses suspended.
>
> There I stayed and I forgot myself,
> My face reclined on the Beloved;
> All ceased and I abandoned myself,
> Leaving my care
> Forgotten among the lilies.

> (*D.N.* st. 6-8)

Into the presence of this love we are, amazingly, not intruders. This is the second reason for John's writing of "the soul" and not "I". He knows that the substance of what he has to say is not merely about himself, but is a shared experience—perhaps realized to some degree already in the reader; perhaps, in the particular forms of contemplation, part of the future development of his spiritual life (*Asc,* Prol. 3). But whether or not these particular forms of experience might be realized in us his readers, John knows that in being dispossessed for Christ he is to be shared out, as Christ is, for all. Beneath the "practical", phenomenal coinciding of experiences—the blessed conversation of one contemplative speaking to another—which even at best must still be partial and fragmentary, there is the totality of his being-for-others. In the Spirit of the Eucharistic Christ ("Take this, all of you . . . which is given for you") and in the image of the Triune God,[9] he makes available to the disposing power of the Spirit even what is most intimate and apparently incommunicable for the good of his brothers and sisters. He keeps nothing of himself for himself. Therefore the "concealment" of the Bride ("I went forth without being observed") is purified of all furtiveness, embarrassment or shame, leaving in this secrecy only the radiant uniqueness of lovers one to another. There is absolutely no need to hide or guard that love, because in this radiance it is quite invulnerable—inscrutable to those who do not share it and the true home of all who do. "The soul", then, means "I", not only John himself in his love of Christ, but each of his readers on the way to God.

Here on earth John could not know how extensive that readership would be.[10] He presumed that his proper audience would be a limited one, confined to those who had entered on the particular ascetical way of monastic life and were being drawn into the experience of contemplative prayer:

> Nor is my principal intention to to address everyone, but certain persons of our holy Order of the Primitive Observance of Mount Carmel, both friars and nuns, whom God is blessing by putting them on the way of this mount.
>
> (*Asc.* Prol, 9)

However, accepting his submission "to better judgement", the Church has amended this view by declaring him to be a Doctor, a teacher, of the whole Church, a singularly valuable guide for all the faithful.[11] There can be no doubt that he is

---

[9] c.f. below pp.

[10] Unlike his true spiritual daughter, Therese of Lisieux, who had a strong intimation of how widely influential the doctrine of her "little way" would be. Shortly before her death, speaking of the eventual publication of her manuscripts, she observed: "There will be something in them for all, except those following extraordinary ways". And a little later: "I feel that my mission is about to begin, my mission of making others love God as I love Him, my mission of teaching my little ways to souls. If God answers my request, my heaven will be spent on earth up to the end of the world. Yes, I want to spend my heaven doing good on earth" (*Story of a Soul*, trans. John Clarke, OCD, I.C.S., Washington, 1976, p 263).

[11] Declared by Pius XI, August 24, 1926.

Doctor mysticus, that his immediate aim and most sublime achievement is to explore the nature of mystical life and to give counsel concerning the dark and delicate ways of responding to that grace. Nor is every person called to live out his Christian vocation in a specifically contemplative mode, with a predominance of mystical gifts. Nevertheless, no one is excluded from this world of grace mediated by St. John. His writings do not belong to a close circle of mystical initiates; every Christian—indeed, every human person—can rightly understand himself to be in some way "the soul" on the way to union of love with God. The mystical intensity does not narrow the way, but rather gives it a universal and cosmic scope. How so? Because John knows that his way can be nothing other than Christ in his death and Resurrection (c.f. *Asc* II, 7, 9). The sublimest contemplation never transcends that mystery of redemption, but simply enters further into the limitless deep caverns of the rock which is Christ (*Cant, 37*) and into the thicket of his Passion, by which God is reuniting all things to Himself (*Ibid,* 36). And John really means all things—the whole universe together and every particular being within it, especially each human person, each "soul, most beautiful among all the creatures" (*Cant* 1:7). God's creative presence and his loving summons to union are never absent from anyone, "not even from a soul in mortal sin" (*Cant* 1:8).

Each reader, then, can certainly understand himself to be "the soul", although this identification will have various modes according to the different contexts. First, and most obviously, there may be an actual identity, the simple recognition of one's own experience in any of the descriptive accounts offered by St. John. These may range from the simply ascetical, such as the incisive exposure of the common faults of "beginners" ranged under the headings of the seven capital vices in Book I of the *Dark Night;* through some of the more common modes of simple contemplative prayer in *Ascent* II or *Dark Night* I; to the more rare experiences of radical purification and illumination in *Dark Night* II, in the latter stanzas of the *Canticle* and in the *Living Flame.* In all of these descriptions John's purpose is the practical concern of a spiritual father.

...There are many other things which befall those who are

following this way: joys, afflictions, hopes and sorrows—
some of which arise from a spirit of perfection, others from
imperfection. With divine help we will seek to say something
of all these, so that each soul that reads this might come to
see the road he is following and the one he should follow if
he intends reaching the summit of this mount.[12]

Two important qualifications should be made here. First,
although it is fair to speak of a common or identical experience, John is nevertheless quite aware of the utterly unique
component in the concrete events of any individual's life.

> It must not be thought that God communicates to everyone
> who reaches this state [Spiritual Espousal] everything which
> is expounded in these two stanzas, nor that he does so in
> one single way and degree of knowledge and feeling.
>
> (*Cant.* 14-15:2)

In no way does he seek to impose the exact timbre of his own
experience as the necessary norm for others, but always defers
to the unique sweet ordering of the Holy Spirit in each person:

> Thus the presence of God is felt sometimes in one way,
> sometimes in another ... and the Lord works thus, who
> infuses as He wills.
>
> (*D.N.* II, 13, 1; 12, 7)

The second observation is by way of caution. One should have
a healthy reserve about too readily interpreting the texts for
oneself and applying them to one's own experience without
the safeguard of conversation with a learned and spiritual
guide. A self-enclosed reading of the text can, with great
sincerity, but also with an insidious grain either of spiritual

---

[12]*Asc.* Prol, 7. c.f. Jacques Maritain's notion of St. John offering a "practically
practical science" of contemplation, reaching into concrete singular circumstances—as
distinct from the "speculatively practical science" of, say, St. Thomas Aquinas, which
is a more general, speculative, explanatory mode of exploring human action. *The
Degrees of Knowledge,* "St. John of the Cross, Practitioner of Contemplation", trans.
Gerald B. Phelan, London, 1959, pp 310-351.

presumption or of discouragement, simply entrench illusion concerning one's spiritual life (c.f. *Asc,* Prol, 6.). Trust in the Holy Spirit should include humble recourse to the living tradition of counsel in the Church:

> He who falls alone, alone stays fallen, and he holds his soul of little account since he entrusts it to himself alone.
>
> (*Sayings of Light and Love,* 8)

Another way of recognizing oneself as "the soul" is by a kind of "foundational identity". John explores not only the phenomena of particular experiences, but also what it means simply to be Christian and to be human. Now, it is of crucial importance to recognize that, in his two-fold purpose "to present and to explain" (*declarar y dar a entender*) contemplative prayer (*Asc,* Prol, 1), it is in the latter, more profound function—that of searching out the *meaning* of mystical phenomena—that he has recourse to the elemental realities of human and Christian existence. To be created in the image of God, with an intrinsic exigence or 'natural desire' to perfect one's personal being through union with God; the darkening of that divine image by sin and the need for purification and illumination; the sheer gift of grace in Christ and the response to that gift in faith, hope and charity; the reality of the energy of the Holy Spirit in the soul and of the sharing of the immanent life of the Holy Trinity—these and other 'basic doctrines' are where St. John finds the source of meaning of all mystical experience. Any Christian—and, according to the universal range of God's saving love, any human person—may recognize himself here. This is what accounts for so many people being able to approach the sublime mystical accounts of the *Canticle* and *Living Flame* not merely with curiosity or 'academic interest', not only with wonder at the awesome heights of sanctity there revealed (so very fitting though that wonder might be), but with a real resonance of shared meaning and a genuine growth in self-understanding. It accounts for that wider 'spiritual ecumenism' by which people from quite different spiritual traditions (including the bleak modern experience of so many individuals apparently alienated from any spiritual tradition) are enlivened and awakened by St. John's experience to the mystical potentialities of their own. It is certainly not that one should fondly imagine that this feeling of sympathy with John's account indicates the actual realization of the mystical gifts in oneself: nevertheless, there is a certain unity or continuity in the whole spectrum of spirituality such that we can speak of an 'analogy of experience'. The innumerable distinct prismatic colours of individual experiences all belong ultimately in the one pure white light of the perfected Church in glory, the heavenly Woman clothed with the sun (Rev 12), the holy city, the new Jerusalem, prepared as a bride adorned for her husband (Rev 21). All the individual colours of human experience have an essential kinship with each other.

✓ For example, when John witnesses to the "living flame of love, that tenderly wounds my soul in its deepest centre", what he has immediately in mind is a very rare experience of mystical transformation: "the soul feeling itself to be wholly enflamed in divine union, its taste wholly bathed in glory and love, and from the innermost depths of its substance to be flowing no less than rivers of glory..." (*L.F.* 1:1). But this complete realization of the capacity for knowledge and love of God— the soul "reaching her last and deepest centre in God" (*L.F.* 1:12)—is the consummation of a long movement, at each moment of which the soul may be said to be "centred" in God.

> As many are the degrees of the love of God that the soul can have, so are the centres that it can have in God, each one being more inward than the other; for the stronger love is more unitive, and in this way we can understand the many mansions which, said the Son of God, were in his Father's house.
>
> (*L.F.* 1:13)

Thus, while one's own experience of love and that of St. John might be very far from identical, they are still not wholly dissociated. When he speaks of the centring power of love in his own sublime mode, each of us can rightly understand it in his own measure, because the essential form of that centring is in every case the same—the mutual indwelling or life-sharing of lover and Beloved, love's intrinsic dynamism towards still greater inwardness, its power to open up to faith-consciousness ever deeper reaches both of the soul and of Christ. This and the other essential features of love—its selflessness, freedom, ardour, tenderness, courage, humility—are all most powerfully manifest in the soul which has arrived at its "deepest centre", but for that very reason they are here most fruitful in revealing to the soul, still at the outer limits, what is the natural goal of its own life. St. John must therefore be read with all the humility and all the hope (the key elements of spiritual realism) that we can bring to bear. He witnesses not to his own achievement but to God's; we ought hear him with an unpretentious openness to whatever gifts of love that same God might choose to bestow, God who is generous unto folly.

Finally, in this Introduction we should give notice of a constant motif that will emerge in our tracing the way of St. John of the Cross, that of "passivity". It is a notion which is profoundly important but also somewhat problematic. Whilst passivity has been commonly held by saints and theologians to be a legitimate feature, or even the crucial defining mark, of maturity in contemplative prayer, it also readily connotes a long series of more or less extravagant and destructive aberrations in Christian spirituality. It was the crux of the issue with the *Alumbrados,* the Illuminists, of St. John's own time in Spain, suspicion of which brought his works before the judgement of the Inquisition in 1622 (where they were successfully defended by the learned Augustinian Fray Basilio Ponce de Leon).[13] Quietists, Beghards, Brethren of the Free Spirit, Cathars, Messalians, Montanists are some of the more notable among a host of sects which have formed around the claim of being illumined and driven by divine inspiration. Again, in the sphere of doctrine as distinct from devotion, the problem of man's relative passivity and activity in response to God's saving intervention has been a constant challenge to theological understanding. The Pelagian, Lutheran and Jansenist controversies mark the critical points in the development of the Church's understanding our dependence upon grace and our

---

[13]E. Allison Peers, *Complete Works,* Vol. I, pp. li ff.; Vol. III, pp. 355-404.

ability to cooperate freely with it.

But the issue of passivity is not merely of historical interest. It is always present in the life of the Church and of every believer, because that life is essentially a shared life with God, a relationship in which giving and receiving are central. The very core of personal existence is involved here, since in this relationship the believer both moves himself out of his own unique resources of knowledge and freedom and (even more!) is *moved by* Him who is calling him into a communion of loving understanding.

At the present time it seems that there is a heightened sense of this dimension of spiritual life. The possibility of manifest divine intervention in "spiritual experiences" is more widely recognized, such intervention more widely expected and even invited. Instruction abounds on the deliberate formation of consciousness or psychological attitude by which such intervention might be received or even elicited. We are in great need of wise counsel here, because passivity as a mode of awareness shares in the vast complexity of human consciousness. Its nuances range from simple inertia or inactivity, as in the spiritual blindness of those who do not care to see, to the saint's most highly refined attentiveness, receptivity and willing exposure to the searching light of God's truth. Passivity may be deliberately chosen and freely cultivated, or it may be an occurrence in which one finds himself, inescapably and without any option, acted upon, "suffering". Moreover, within that situation of his being moved, the quality of his response may be more or less passive—he may ignore the phenomenon or resist it, consent or surrender to it. John of the Cross is a master of discernment of these things. Not only is he able to give an astute phenomenological description of the many kinds of inner experience, but he reveals a certain form and pattern among them by which their deeper spiritual value as communion with God might be judged. Although passivity is usually, and quite rightly, associated with advanced degrees of the spiritual life and of mystical prayer in particular, John can show us how certain modes of passivity have their necessary place at every state of the spiritual ascent, including the very beginning. Passivity can thus provide an integrating thread for the whole course of spiritual growth. Through this perspective St. John enables us to estimate to what extent the higher reaches of mystical union are, on the one hand, privileged and extraordinary, and, on the other, are the proper fulfillment in this life of God's gift of Himself in the grace of Christ.

2

Creation—"By the Hand of the Beloved"

My Beloved, the mountains,
The solitary wooded valleys,
The strange islands,
The sonorous rivers,
The whisper of the loving breezes,

The tranquil night
At the time of the rising of the dawn,
The silent music,
The sounding solitude
The supper that recreates and enkindles love.

(*Cant.* 14-15)

John of the Cross was an ardent lover of the beauty of God's creation. It is one of the most constant themes in his companions' witness about him. He rejoiced in the bounty of nature with that particular clarity of perception born of habitual, simply-accepted frugality; from a childhood with a poor widowed mother who could give him just sufficient food and abundant tender affection, to the chosen austerity of monastic observance. The large sweep of landscape enthralled him and made his journeys a joy—across the vast spare plains of Castile and Ciudad Real, through the grandeur of the Sierras Guadarrama, de Segura and Nevada, in the astounding lushness of the garden valleys of Andalusia. He had an artisan's love of embodying form: as Prior of the monastery of Los Martires near Granada he had built a strong, rhythmically— arched aqueduct and an elegant cloister soft-shadowed for recollection. He had a fine sensibility for small things, whether a wildflower or a bird from nature's hand or a carved crucifix from his own. The harmony of sound was innate in him; poetry and music readily came to his lips to celebrate the beauty of God and the Virgin Mother of God. The beauty of the world was native to him: by God's grace he made it native to his life with God.

St. John does not offer an ordered treatise specifically devoted to creation. Nevertheless, on virtually every page of his writings there is reference to it; or, more correctly, to "them", *las criaturas*—we enter a realm not of generalized, abstract doctrine, but of individual beings and actual spiritual experience. It is also a situation of disturbing paradox.

For St. John's attitude to creation might at first sight appear to be ambiguous or even contradictory. There is ample evidence to support both poles of a double image: that of the intransigently austere ascetic who searches after God alone through an exclusion of all else in a "going forth from all things which is done by abhorring and despising them" (*Cant* 1:20). Even in this "going forth" John is never anything but lyrical, but what he is celebrating is the terrible beauty and purity of the "nothing", *nada,* of total renunciation (*Asc* I, 13, 11). On the other hand, there is the rapturous visionary and poet who exults in the sublime beauty of creation, who "feels and knows the truth of that saying which St. Francis uttered, namely, 'God mine and all things'" (*Cant.* 14:5), and whose vision inspired some of the most splendid and delicately sensuous verses of all Spanish poetry.

There can be no denying the force of either of these faces of St. John's spirituality. What we must find is the single coherent view that will include both of them. Perhaps we should declare at the outset that the tension is a genuine intellectual, doctrinal issue, and that an adequate explanation of it must likewise be theological: it would be quite beside the point to attempt to reduce the polarities to a psychological account of 'personality tension', as though the 'nature poet' in him is in conflict with the drive of religious other-worldliness, or the 'liberated mystic' is breaking through the dogmatic shackles of the scholastic theologian. Such spiritual double-mindedness is a travesty of the man and his doctrine. On the contrary, we can perceive in him a marvelous integrity which is able to contain and meaningfully relate both radical renunciation and profuse celebration of creaturely good. That wholeness rests upon St. John's fundamental principle of the spiritual life, namely, God's absolute transcendence, and the correlative total dependence of creation.

Our first step towards that coherent view will be to grasp the nettle of his unsparing declarations of the "nothingness" of creatures and the necessity of detachment. There follows its dialectical counterpart in the goodness and beauty of creation which, by its continuous derivation from God, can lead man on to the transcendent Source of all value. Finally, because the recreation of man and his spiritual illumination is through the grace of Christ, and that same Christ is the one in whom all things are sustained, it follows that St. John's highest mystical vision gives a glimpse of how the natural dependence or passivity of all creation is itself being transformed (though commonly hidden under the veil of faith) to share in the glorious freedom of the children of God.

> This is the adoption of the sons of God, who truly will say to God what the Son himself said to the Eternal Father through St. John: 'All of mine are yours and all of yours are mine' (Jn 17:10).
>
> *(Cant.* 36:5)

The "Nothingness" of Creation

A perennial trend of human religious sensibility, especially of the mystical tradition, is the desire for an ultimate unity. Not infrequently that goal of unity has been envisaged as the absorption of the contemplative's individuality into a single ground of Being, in which 'perfect' state the apparent multiplicity of all created beings is seen to dissolve into the One. Diversity among beings is lamented as fragmentation, distinction as tragic separation and alienation. It is therefore especially important to understand correctly what St. John of the Cross means in his vigorous assertion of the "nothingness" of creatures and his insistence that they be "left aside" for the sake of divine union.

> And since every creature whatsoever, and all of its actions and abilities, cannot conformed or attain to that which God is, therefore the soul must be stripped of every creature and of its own actions and abilities ... so that when all that is unlike to God and unconformed to him is cast out, the soul is thus transformed in God.
>
> (*Asc,* II, 5, 4)

In this passage we can see how St. John builds his practical doctrine of prayer upon the foundation of the nature of objective reality: "And *since* every creature ...*therefore* the soul must...." If, therefore, he is to be acquitted of Monist or pantheist leanings, it cannot be by dismissing the problematic language as merely incautious and inexact rhetoric about subjective techniques. St. John has a studied theological view of the meaning of the created world, and he will not divorce the subjective features of the soul's ascent from that wider context. Again, his unremitting *via negativa* cannot be completely explained merely as the rejection of sinful involvement with creatures. Although that purification from sin is an essential feature, which we must examine in due course, there is still a more fundamental, purely ontological ground to his constant drive of absolute transcendence in prayer.

That ground is the unassailable transcendence of God over his whole creation. However much John might celebrate the value of creatures in the lyricism of his poetry and the sensuousness of much of his prose, he will never jeopardize God's unique holiness by making him continuous with this finite reality, even as its consummation and crown.

> For although it is true that all creatures have, as theologians say, a certain relation to God and a trace of God ... yet there is no essential likeness or connection between them and God; rather, the distance between their being and his divine Being is infinite.
>
> (*Asc.* II, 8, 3)

Here he gives passing acknowledgement of the positive aspect of the "analogy of being", that is, that the being, goodness, truth and beauty of creatures is a reflection or trace of the absolute source of these values in God. However, he is far more inclined to insist upon the negative corollary to the analogy, epitomized in the statement of the Fourth Lateran Council (1215): "Between the Creator and the creature there can be no likeness perceived which is not surpassed by a greater unlikeness between them".[1] As the unoriginate source of all meaning, God can never be included within any overarching category of being, beauty, goodness or wisdom; there can be no horizon beyond God within which perspective he might be measured, "since God falls within no genus and no species, whereas creatures do" (*Asc.* III, 12, 1). Reverence for that absolute holiness of God is what inspires John's emphatic denial of any "proportion" between Creator and creature (*Asc.* II, 8, 3; III, 12, 1), and so there can be no reciprocal relationship through which God's perfection might derive its meaning from what he has made. In this quite literal sense, John affirms God to be "incomparable", "incomprehensible" (*Ibid*). Seen in this light, John's language is not at all extravagant, even when he speaks of a certain infinite gulf between God and all else: "God is of another being (*de otro ser*) than his creatures in that he is infinitely far from them all" (*Asc.* III, 12, 2).

The reverse side of God's absolute transcendence is the total dependence of creation. Because God is the self-sufficient fullness of Being, and creatures in their finitude are quite unlike or "infinitely remote" from him, St. John perceives that in this respect they are virtually nothing: "All the being of creatures compared with the infinite Being of God, is nothing" (*Asc.* I 4, 4). A creature does not alongside against God as independently possessing with him a share in the further horizon of Being. God himself is always ultimate, and whatever exists of finite meaning and value can only be flowing *from* the divine fullness. Here we must recall how often St. John names not only "the

---

[1] Inter creatorem et creaturam non potest tanta similitudo notari quin inter eos maior sit dissimilitudo notanda. *D-S*, 806.

creatures", but also "their actions and abilities" as that which is other than God and dependent on him. It follows that the most perfect of all created reality—a spiritual creature's free gift of himself in love back to God—has its ultimate source in God's creative power:

> All the goodness that we have is lent to us and God holds it to be his own; it is God at work, and his work is God.
>
> (*Points of Love,* 29)

The "nothingness" of creation, then, is St. John's strongest way of expressing its absolute dependence or passivity under God's sustaining action. Of itself, apart from God, creation has nothing and can be nothing.

It is clear that he experienced this truth not merely as detached, cool, metaphysical speculation, but as the actual living quality of his own and the world's existence. "Creation" means for him primarily the ongoing divine conservation of things, and he heightens that truth dramatically by reflecting that only thus is the creature being held out of annihilation.

> God dwells and is present substantially in every soul, even in the greatest sinner in the world. And this kind of union is always being wrought between God and all creatures, for in it he is conserving their being; and in such a way that if it were to fail them, they would at once be annihilated and would leave off being.
>
> (*Asc.* II, 5, 3)

Everything created is continuously receiving its being from God. It is an awesome perception, directed not so much to the cosmic scope of the truth as to the individual person, *el alma,* and his particular concrete circumstances; not so much to the consequent substantial reality of his contingent being as to the sheer dependence, almost the precariousness, of his existence. The possibility of not being is an aspect of creaturely existence which leavens St. John's perception of the world with a certain holy fear. We must therefore have care not to fall into the anachronism of imagining his intuition of the natural beauty of woods and mountains, of meadows enamelled with flowers, of nights more lovely than the dawn, to be that of nineteenth-century Romanticism, which at least implicity would hold numinous Nature to be an Absolute. The "nothingness" of creation would then be merely an extrinsic doctrinaire post-script to his original "mystical" vision, a moralistic caution on the transience of perceived beauty. St. John's is not a two-tiered experience of beautiful natural perception and severe theological proviso. On the contrary, his very perception of creatures is itself theological: "*the creatures* make answer to the soul" (*Cant.* 5:1). The soul "hears" and "sees" them to be *in themselves (en si)* entirely receptive of their being, wholly pointing away from themselves. It is not surprising that he should here recall the testimony of St. Augustine, in whose experience of creatures he recognizes his own: "And they cried out with loud voice, 'God made us'" (*Cant.* 5:1; *Confessions,* Bk X, ch. vi).

His perception in creatures of their possible non-being determines the nature of St. John's quest for God. One would normally expect the idea of the immanent creative presence of God to invite reflection on the goodness of created things and their spiritual blessing for man. That indeed is the initial line he follows in the passage from the *Spiritual Canticle.* But granted his dominant viewpoint of divine transcendence, it is not perverse nor even paradoxical, but perfectly consistent, that in the *Ascent of Mount Carmel* he should immediately turn such an allusion to the divine presence into an exhortation to ascetic denial.

> The more a soul is wrapped up in creatures and its own abilities by habit and affection, so much the less disposition it has for union [with God]. The soul, then, needs only to strip itself of these natural dissimilarities and contrarieties, so that God, who is communicating himself naturally to it through the way of nature, might communicate himself supernaturally through grace.
>
> (*Asc,* II, 5, 4)

As the uncreated Source of all created being, God is unique, and so the soul's authentic quest for God must be a quest for God alone. Such, then, is the meaning of the "nothingness" of creatures and its consequence in the spiritual life. It is not meant to be a term of denigration; it simply affirms as a matter of fact the absolute transcendence of God and the intrinsic transcending quality of the soul's quest for him. It is a cogent argument, and St. John clearly values this richer understanding of the ascetical life through relating it to the ontological structure of creation. But we must also remember that for St. John the vital truth of this ascetic way depends on its being not simply the implementation of a religious philosophy, but a response in faith to Christ's summons:

> For this reason Our Lord, teaching us this way, said through St. Luke: . . . 'He that does not renounce all that he possesses [with his will] cannot be my disciple' (Lk 14:33). And this is evident, for the doctrine which the Son of God came to teach was the leaving aside (*menosprecio,* literally 'less-valuing') of all things so that one might be able to receive in himself the reward (*precio,* 'value') of the Spirit of God.
>
> (*Asc* I, 5, 2; II, 6, 4: III, 7, 2; L.F. 3:46)

That the way of dispossession is in harmony with the nature of being is indeed a great part of its blessing, but even that is simply a fruit of the more radical harmony of accepting the wisdom of the Son of God.

We turn now to a more difficult issue. There are several passages which, taken in their apparent obvious meaning, are quite repellent. Understood thus, they would rightly be disowned by the psychologically healthy and orthodox Christian. It is well to deal with them squarely. To censor them out of our image of John of the Cross through distaste or an embarrassed attmept to save our saints reputation would in principle be dishonest. And, what is more, it would in fact be a mistake, an opportunity lost for an ultimately more humane understanding of the man.

And so, closely interwoven with the simple metaphysical exigence towards detachment, there is another thread, a much more strident demand, in which the negative aspect of creation becomes harshly stated. Parallel to the being (or nothingness) of creatures compared with the Being of God, "all the beauty of creatures, compared with the infinite beauty of God, is the height of deformity", their grace is the height of misery and ugliness, their goodness "may be described as wickedness", the world's wisdom "pure and supreme ignorance", and so with liberty and slavery, delight and affliction, wealth and poverty, glory and misery (*Asc.* I, 4, 4). Whatever perfection we might discern in creatures, "compared with" the same perfection in God it becomes in some way its opposite evil. We are here confronted not so much with creation's total dependence on God, as its seeming opposition to his holiness.

The problem is compounded by a further passage in which St. John violently contrasts the "evil" of creatures, not with the unique holiness of God, but with the beauty and nobility of the soul!

> There is more difference between excellence of soul and the best of creatures than there is between clear diamond or fine gold and pitch.
>
> (*Asc,* I, 9, 1)

Can this be an echo of a much earlier Spanish spirituality, that associated with Priscillian, bishop of Avila (c. 380), in which there is a strong Gnostic Dualism of spirit and matter as good and evil, and in which the soul is an emanation from the Godhead, disastrously united to a body as punishment for sin? Does it suggest that corporeality is to be abhorred, rather than contigency simply acknowledged? That attitude might seem to be present even more clearly in a further sentence, whose ambiguity seems so far to have escaped the notice of St. John's commentators:

> and there is more difference between the soul and the rest of corporeal creatures (*las demas criaturas corporales*) than between a highly clarified liquor and mire most foul (*Ibid*).

One possible reading of this passage, probably favoured by the Spanish syntax, is the orthodox Catholic one by which the soul is one *among* "the rest of corporeal creatures"—the soul being "corporeal" in the sense of being intrinsically united to the body as form to matter and, in spite of its own specific immateriality, different from the simply spiritual being of angels. However, another possible reading could distinguish the soul as spiritual and immaterial *from* "other, corporeal, creatures". The immaterial would thus be identified with purity, the bodily with filth. Unhappily, the extended metaphor might well suggest such a reading—the soul clinging to other creatures is like a pure liquid defiled with mud (*Ibid*). And finally, the dark shadow of dualism might be suspected in the rhetorical horrors with which John tries to describe a soul so defiled— things filled with cobwebs, with worms, even the corruption of a dead body, are not so filthy (*Ibid*). Is this the kind of passionate revulsion which characterizes an obsessive, morbidly spiritualist conception of purity?

A preliminary step in answer to this problem should be to place it in its proper cultural context. The true temper of this kind of reflection must be sought in the perspective of sixteenth-century piety, which, unlike our own clinically sanitized view, was more accustomed to facing the harsh facts of physical suffering and decay. These were a far more frequent and obstrusive part of ordinary life, and John's culture was far more capable than ours of reflecting on them within a creative ascetical context and thus without morbid obsession.

Nevertheless, the principal answer must lie in something more secure than cultural style. The key is to recognize that St. John consistently ascribes these dreadful abominations to "unruly desires" or "disordered passion". That is, he offers a searching exposition of *moral* evil, not opposed ontological principles of good and evil within creation. Just as gold or diamond, if heated and placed upon pitch, is stained by it, "just so the soul which is hot with desire for any creature draws forth uncleanness from it through the heat of its desire and is stained by it" (*Asc.* I, 9, 1). Deferring for a moment the objection that the creature itself still seems to be source of evil—the "diamond" is placed upon "pitch"—it is clear that the immediate effective cause of the foulness is the subjective "heat of desire". And because it is a truly moral, spiritual issue, John assures us that he is not speaking of spontaneous sensuous desires—these "hinder the soul little, if at all, from attaining to union" (*Asc* I, 11, 2) but of deliberate, free commitment.[2] The natural inclination or "first movement" of sensitive appetite is in itself no absolute impediment, even though it might manifest the lack of integrity of fallen human nature when, as concupiscence, its own independent vitality heads towards an immediate sensuous gratification quite at variance with authentic good which that person may simultaneously be willing (*Ibid*). No; the terrible "disorder" which John laments consists in a person reducing the properly infinite capacity of his spirit to mere contingency, "when he fulfills the appetite of his will (*cumple el apetito de su voluntad*) in any creature" (*Asc.* I, 9, 1). It is not the loving of a creature which is wrong, but the idolatry in that futile "fulfilling" of the spirit with anything other than God.

This true ascetical meaning of evil becomes more apparent in St. John's bold affirmation that no degree of moral evil, for all that it might disfigure and blaspheme the God-given natural goodness of the soul, can radically destroy it:

> the disordered soul in its natural being is as perfect as when God created it, yet in its rational being it is vile, abominable, foul, dark and full of all evils.
>
> (*Asc.* I, 9, 3)

Turning the tables on our earlier suspicions, the "natural being" of the soul, which presumably includes the sensuous dimension of human life, retains its intrinsic goodness in spite of the degradation of its spiritual capacity (*el ser de razon*) through the disordered "desire of the will". It is for this reason that we need not fear that the violent antitheses which characterize

---

[2]It might seem strange to a modern reader that St. John should place this reassurance concerning natural sensitive appetite so late (chapt. 11) in his ascetical discourse. In our post-Jansenistic age we are liable to be dismayed at the harsh things he has to say concerning "desires" in his earlier chapters, fearing that he is vilifying mere natural sensibility. That he should not feel it necessary to "explain himself" from the outset, may well indicate that he does not even envisage our kind of anxiety and defensiveness concerning sensuous life. Quite the opposite of harshness and suspicion concerning these "natural movements", he would appear, for all his ascetical rigour, to have a fundamental implicit assumption of their validity in human, Christian living.

John's ascetical doctrine manifest anything other than a Castilian's relish for the spiritual combat. For all the vehemence of his language, redemption is still primarily not destruction but transformation, in which

> to him that is pure, all things, whether high or low, work for greater good and serve for greater purity.
>
> (*Asc.* III, 16, 6).

We have yet to face the difficulty that, whilst the subjective moral disorder is the cause of the soul's sinful condition, must there not be some sense in which the creature itself remains a source of evil for the soul? We must therefore consider more closely what St. John means by the creature "compared with" the being and goodness of God. A comparison is usually made by a kind of mental separation of beings set one over against the other, a presuming that they each possess complete and mutually independent existences—the kind of clear confrontation implied in "the fact that all that the soul grants to the creature, it takes from God" (*Asc.* III, 12, 1). It is indeed true that all perfection belongs to God in a unique and infinite mode which makes him "completely other": but this otherness must not be reversed to imply the complete autonomy of creaturely being from the Being of God. Such a notion is quite illusory, for creation can exist, as we have seen, only by a continuous dynamic dependence upon God—"if union of this kind were to fail them, they would at once leave off being" (*Asc.* II, 5, 3). Therefore, in the moral-ascetical context, a false kind of comparison which assumes complete autonomy of creation is 'unreal' in a most literal sense, corresponding to "nothing". To regard a creature not just as subsistent, but wholly subsistent of itself, denying at least implicitly that it is received as a crumb from the table of God (*Asc.* I, 6, 3), that it is present at all only as a trace of the passing of God (*Cant.* 5:3), this in fact is to attempt to approach it as separated from the very source of its being, beauty, goodness, truth, etc. Sin is the illusion involved in insisting on that unreal kind of separation even though God is literally "imcomparable", not to be compared with his creatures set over against him. In as much as a person grasps at a creature in this false, alienating way, he destroys its true value for himself as a mediation of the unique Source of all value.

> When the soul distances itself from God through deliberate affection for a creature, there come upon it all evils and disasters to the extent of the pleasure and affection with which it joins itself to the creature; for this is inherent in withdrawal from God.
>
> *(Asc.* III, 19, 1)

By a tragic irony, the very perfections of creation can become occasions of evil for the soul when their passivity under God's conserving action is lost to sight.

We ought to remark that this error concerning the relationship between God and his creatures is not simply an intellectual mistake. More important than any conceptual formulation, it can be an attitude of heart, an evil which comes upon the soul, a quality of a person's life. Here is a powerful example of a how a doctrinal question—creation's passivity under God—is perceived by St. John of the Cross to be a concrete "practical" issue in the spiritual life.

> For it is a very easy thing to judge of the Being and greatness of God less worthily and nobly than befits his incomprehensibility. For although reason and judgement might form no express conception that God is like any of these [ideas and images given in mystical prayer], yet the very esteeming of these things ... makes the soul not to esteem God nor feel towards him as highly as faith teaches us—that he is incomparable, incomprehensible, etc.
>
> *(Asc.* III, 12, 1)

Whatever might be the extent and rightness (or otherwise) of a person's theological speculation, St. John requires an existential knowledge or conviction (*juzgar*) of divine transcendence in the fabric of fundamental attitudes and the unformulated subtleties of actual living—"in the inwardness of the soul" (*Ibid*).

John's own intention in writing of the "nothingness" of

creation is likewise aimed at actual spiritual life. He offers little in the way of a speculative exploration of the analogy of being, but he hopes to guide us into a living discernment of creation's dependence on God in such a way that, in the very experience of natural beauty, one "will direct his heart to God with delight and joy, because God is in himself all these beauties and graces in the most eminent degree and is infinitely high above all created things" (*Asc.* III, 21, 2).

On a plausible but mistaken reading, this aspect of his teaching might seem to reflect only a harsh insensibility—apart from God, "grace and beauty are the smoke and vapour of the earth" (*Ibid*). In fact, however, it offers a tremendous enrichment in human spiritual living: an encounter with creaturely grace and beauty should be the occasion of the spirit opening in genuine freedom and happiness by receiving them with gratitude, not grasping at them, and by discerning the divine generosity behind them—". . . to give thanks to God who gives them in order to be better known and loved" (*Asc.* III, 21, 1). If a person is free from grasping blind desire, he is able to discern creatures in their constant total passivity under God, and as coming to himself from the hand of God. To regard them so, carries that objective passivity of creatures into his own spiritual life as grateful receptivity. The "nothingness" or total dependence of a creature is in fact the mode of its genuine God-given value, and thus it becomes for the one who so perceives it the vehicle of a divine enrichment.

> If you purify your soul of alien possessions and desires you will understand things in spirit; and if you deny your desire for them, you will delight in them in their truth, understanding what is sure in them.
>
> (*Sayings,* 47)

Finally, then, we can already perceive a profound integrity of joyful asceticism in St. John. It is not as though a prevailing attitude of severe disparagement of creatures is occasionally relieved by an alternate phase of benign celebration. The way of spiritual poverty—"having nothing" (c.f. 2 Cor. 6:10)—

generates its own transfigured joy. To "let them go" in effective detachment is the only way of attaining the authentic goodness of created things.

> This man then rejoices in all things—by not having a possessive joy in them—as if he had them all.... Having none of them in his heart, he possesses them all, as St. Paul says, in great freedom.
>
> *(Asc.* III, 20, 3)

"Scattering a Thousand Graces": The Goodness of Creation

So far we have seen how St. John's doctrine of creation, with its strong sense of the absolute transcendence of God, has a negative corollary in the "nothingness" of creatures and their openness to non-existence should God's sustaining presence be withdrawn. Positively, however, this radical dependence leads not to an attitude of anxiety or St.oic disdain, as if creation were ultimately futile. Rather, St. John perceives its finitude and transience with a great compassion, with a heightened sense of reverence for God's tender care in conserving it, and for the dynamism inherent in its very existence through a union "continually being wrought" *(Asc.* II, 5, 3).

This positive value of creation emerges strongly in stanzas four and five of the *Spiritual Canticle*:

> O woods and thickets
> planted by the hand of the Beloved:
> O meadow of verdure
> enamelled with flowers:
> Say if he has passed by you.
>
> Scattering a thousand graces
> he passed by these groves in haste,
> and gazing on them as he went,
> with his reflection alone
> left them clothed with beauty.

It is "with a special awareness" *(advertidamente)* that the soul sings of the woods and thickets—the natural order—being planted by the hand of the Beloved. For although God does many things through the mediation of other creatures, "this action, which is to create, he has never done, nor does he do it, except through his own hand. And so the soul is greatly moved to love her Beloved, God" (*Cant.* 4:3). There is here a two-fold immediacy of God to his creation. Firstly, the small interpolation of the present tense, "nor does he do it", shows that John recognizes God's creative act to be an historically present reality. That God "left in them some trace" and "bestowed on them innumerable graces" (*Cant.* 5:1) cannot be taken in the Deist sense of God's establishing the world in the beginning and leaving it to its built-in devices. He remains its support at every moment of its existence, and therefore the soul's living relationship with the Creator through contemplation of nature is not just a 'memory' of that vastly remote instant of creation's first appearing. One is involved in an immediate present mystery, for the Beloved is creating still.

The immediacy is not only temporal but also ontological. The act of creation cannot be delegated to any other hands, not to any secondary created cause. For the difference between existence and non-existence can lie only within the power of one who not merely receives or shares in being, but is himself its very fount: "God created all things with great facility and brevity; . . . he gave them being out of nothing" (*Cant.* 5:1). And so, paradoxically, it is the "infinite distance" between the absolute Being of God and the contingency of all creatures which is the very reason, in another sense, of his immediate presence to them. The "distance" denotes the uniqueness of God's utter self-sufficiency, so wholly unlike the creature's being which can only be received. But that unique self-possession of God is the condition of his being the source of all else and, if unique, then also the *immediate* source of every creature, since no other being can possibly be charged with the essentially divine power of creating. This is that "substantial union" by which God is present in the inmost reach of every creature, giving it life and being (*Asc.* II, 5, 3; *Cant.* 1:6; 11:3).

Morever, because of God's very nature, St. John perceives his creative presence as deeply personal—immediacy is therefore a matter of intimacy:

> the soul has its natural and radical life, as do all created things, in God, according to the word of St. Paul who says, 'In him we live and move and are'. . . . And St. John says that all that was made was life in God.
>
> > (*Cant.* 8:3; Acts 17:28; Jn 1:4).

Even though personal presence is completed only in the mutual relationship of love and knowledge between spiritual beings, there is nevertheless a certain vitality running through the whole of creation. It is not even confined to those beings which have intrinsic power of self-movement—plants, animals and spiritual creatures—but belongs to all things (*todas las cosas criadas*) including the merely material. Simply in virtue of their existing, they are signs of a living presence of God. And so, St. John's awesome point of departure in the absolute transcendence of God issues in a deep reverence for the sheer fact of creaturely existence—the wonder that things should be at all in face of possible nothingness.

There is another dimension to his contemplation of nature, more accessible, warm, humane. It relishes the richness of creaturely being, *what* it is, its essence. The marvel is not just that it should exist, but that it should exist *thus*:

> not only did he gives them being out of nothing, but he even endowed them with innumerable graces and virtues, making them beautiful with a marvellous order and unfailing dependence among themselves.
>
> > (*Cant.* 5:1)

The "existential" contemplation of nature gives rise in a single penetrating insight to the religious awe at God's power giving these things being out of nothing: but this is interwoven with the "essential" aspect of being, whose largesse unfolds in a more discursive mediation, and it qualifies God's sheer creative power by his loving care and 'nurture':

> These varieties and wonders could be made and nurtured (*criar* rather than *crear*!) only by the hand of the beloved God.
>
> > (*Cant.* 4:3)

Although there can be "no proportion" or "no essential resemblance" between God and creatures in regard to the intrinsic power of existing, yet, once granted the creatures' being, then their intelligibility, goodness and beauty reflect something of the infinite bounty of the Creator—"the creatures are a kind of trace of the passing of God" (*Cant.* 5:3). This is the reason why John perceives the passivity of created being not just as a radical dependence for very existence, but as a continuous enrichment and fulfillment.

For St. John of the Cross, that richness of creation is manifest primarily in the form of beauty. Whilst he recognizes other transcendental values of being, goodness and truth, it is the luminous quality of the beautiful irradiating creatures which so fascinates him in his contemplative quest. Words such as beauty, form, order, variety and diversity, enliven every page of the *Spiritual Canticle,* so much so that his whole spirituality might be taken as a virile and religiously transformed aesthetic. Pre-eminent among all created forms is the beauty of the human person: "O soul, most beautiful of all the creatures..." (*Cant.* 1:7). Taking up the idea of the soul as the image of God, he seizes upon its aesthetic implications and develops them in his ascetical doctrine.

> In the same way that traces of soot would defile a face that is most perfect and complete, so in that way do disordered desires foul and defile the soul that has them, which is in itself a most beautiful and complete image of God.
>
> (*Asc.* I, 9, 1)

Sin is the disfigurement of something essentially lovely. It evokes in St. John a vivid sorrow or grieving, far removed from harsh judgement and censoriousness. It is as though his view of the human person and the cultivation there of the divine likeness is a transference into the spiritual realm of his exquisite sensuous artistry. This artisan of the soul also traced the compelling little sketch of his 'Cristo', Christ on the cross, with such delicate line and vertiginous perspective. The same hand was often engaged in carving poor wood into finely wrought images of the Crucified. Only such a sensitivity which is at once theological, pastoral and aesthetic can account for his extraordinarily vehement and prolonged attack in the *Living Flame* upon misguided spiritual directors (*L.F.* 3:42-62), who blunder ahead "according to their own way and the manner suitable to themselves" (para 46), who know only of "hammering and pounding with the faculties like a blacksmith" (para 43), and who thus "offer a great insult and contempt to God by laying their coarse hands where God is working" (para 54). Clear-sighted and full-blooded outrage! Once again, here in the sphere of spiritual direction, disaster can be traced to a failure to obey the law of selflessness, when the director imposes his own closed perceptions in a region which calls for reverence, humility and docility to the Spirit.

Besides the beauty of the soul itself which is being restored to the likeness of God, the creation in which it cannot fail to be interwoven is also perceived in terms of beauty, and that on a cosmic scale. St. John's contemplative view traverses all the different spheres of created reality in a classical cosmology: from the highest angelic orders, reaching through their descending ranks to man, the meeting place of spirit and matter; thence to the lower creatures—animals, fish, birds, plants—and the primal elements of fire, air, earth, water; all is knit together in an unfailing coherence and integrity (c.f. *Cant.* 5:1-3). The quite different explorations of Copernicus and Galileo were about to dissolve these tradional "spheres" of Western imagination and hurl man into the unimaginable material vastness and complexity of modern science, but John of the Cross seems to retain the implicit security and order of traditional cosmology. Nevertheless, it is most important to bear in mind his passionate aesthetic response to form if we are to judge truly of his frequently allusions to order and hierarchy. They are not the marks of a cold and rigid formalism, but of a delight in the inner radiance of harmony and design. Creation is not only from God's sovereign might, but also "through his Wisdom" (*Cant.* 5:1), a fertile, gentle and infinitely ingenious Wisdom which is revealed as he "passes with great facility", "scattering a thousand graces".

St. John's perception of created beauty is therefore of an extraordinary integrity and wholeness, spanning the whole range from matter to spirit. Indeed, it is a mark not just of his artistry, but of his sanctity, that he should manifest in himself the central illuminating mystery of the Incarnation, by which the flesh embodies and becomes translucent to the Spirit. This is why it is so important not to fragment and distort his work (and his person) by dissociating his poetry and his prose commentaries from each other: the intellectual light of his doctrine has as its proper home the warm lyric sensuousness, the tender ardent eros of his poetry. He makes no disjunction between matter and spirit. Sensuous beauty is not a trace thrown away after God's passing, but is truly sacramental of His beautiful presence. The form or harmony which shines out in created beauty is a refraction of the one true Form, divine Wisdom, which is continuously irradiating not just the individual object itself, but the whole fabric of creation, weaving it together in a vital harmony—illuminating Wisdom, "flowing down from God through the first hierarchies even to the last, and thence to men" (*D.N.* II, 12, 3). Moreover, this mediation through the angelic hierarchies is true not only of the downward movement of God's gracious creativity, but also of creation's ascent to God: ". . . the hierarchies and choirs of angels, through whom from choir to choir our sighs and prayers go to God" (*Cant.* 2:3). We ought to recall that St. John is quite explicit in reserving the very act of creation to God alone, even at the heart of ongoing conservation. But in the gifts of Providence and grace by which God draws creation together and upwards to himself, there is a continuous communion from one order of being to the next. Moreover, that order or design is not merely decorative; just as the sun's ray is modified as it passes through ordered layers of glass, so the whole design of creation adapts the pure and otherwise intolerably powerful divine gift to each creature's frail capacity to receive (c.f. *D.N.* II, 12, 3). St. John thus perceives the beautiful design or 'grace' of creation as sacramental of God's tender "gracious" care.

This aesthetic mode of perceiving the creature's God-given value therefore conditions St. John's contemplative understanding of the Creator himself. He is revealed not just as the Source of contingent being, to which beauty is consequently attributed by man as an accidental ornament. God creates the beautiful as truly as he creates beings: he is the fullness of

Beauty as truly as he is of Being.

> In the living contemplation and understanding of creatures
> the soul sees that they have such abundance of graces and
> virtues and beauty with which God has endowed them, that
> they appear to her to be all clothed with a wonderful natural
> beauty and virtue, derived from and communicated by that
> infinite supernatural beauty of the image (*figura*) of God,
> whose beholding of them clothes the world and all the
> heavens with beauty and happiness.

>   (*Cant.* 6:1)

St. John has here made a peculiar and very beautiful transposition. Theological tradition had long observed that all
creation has its being as the effect of God's creative knowledge—"of all creatures, both spiritual and corporeal, it is not
because they are that therefore God knows them; rather, therefore they are because God knows them".[3] Again, all created
goodness is the effect, not the cause, of God's love for it-"the
love of God is infusing and creating goodness in things" (*S.T.*
I, 20, 2, c.). All of this, of course, is a sheer reversal of human
knowing and loving, which is *moved by* the object's being and
goodness. John now transposes this pattern to the aesthetic
realm. The divine "gave" (*mirar*) actually forms the created
beauty. God is the original Contemplative whose delighted,
living gaze bestows on all things their beauty:

>   and gazing on them as he went,
>   with his reflection alone
>   left them clothed with beauty.

>   (*Cant* 5)

By representing the divine creative action in this way, rather
than as the painstaking care of the artisan, John brilliantly
weds the notions of total power and utter delicacy and finesse.
In this way, once again, creation's total dependence upon God's
action is perceived not as constraint, not as an unhappy subjec-

---

[3]Augustine, *De Trin,* XV, 13; Thomas Aquinas, *S.T.* I, 14, 8.

tion to an alien domination, but as a wonderful gratuitous privilege.

There is another theological asset in this model of God as the original Contemplative: it makes for a kind of continuity between God's creative purpose and man's natural contemplation. For if created beauty is the immediate effect of God's creative gaze, then man's perception of that beauty and his sharing in its substantial joy will be a meeting precisely with the mediated gaze and joy of God. Thus, at the beginning of his discussion of the contemplation of nature, John alludes to the Pauline doctrine that "the invisible things of God are known by the soul through the created visible and invisible things" (*Cant* 4:1; Rom 1:20). Under the pressure of his own religious sensibility, John again makes his aesthetic transposition: instead of remaining with the rather indeterminate notion of "things", he elaborates St. Paul's suggestion in the form of a passionate response to the upward call of beauty.

> The soul, wounded in love by this trace of her Beloved which she has known from the creatures, yearns to see that invisible Beauty which has caused this visible beauty.
>
> (*Cant.* 6:1)

That sacramental quality of creation is of vital importance for understanding St. John's natural contemplation. He does not rest upon the finite beauty in a simply natural aesthetic gaze, at the same time making a kind of conceptual reservation that this is only a sign of some higher value. "Contemplation" for St. John always means *in living faith*: the vital centre of his perception of natural beauty is the "yearning to behold that invisible Beauty". The creature is the immediate finite "place" where transcendent Beauty itself is discerned. Thus, even though the contemplation of created beauty is indeed a real joy and fruition; it bears within itself an even stronger movement of restless self-transcendence.

Here, then, is a profound kind of renunciation, but different from the simple, resolute disciplining of inappropriate desire. Because created beauty is wholly from God, the most authentic experience of it will recognize that dependence which is intrinsic to its very nature, and will spontaneously reach out towards its living Source. Such a renunciation is elicited *by* the very natural beauty which is contemplated; indeed, it is a continuation and the proper fulfillment of *ecstasis* towards beauty, a movement "through" the creature as an authentic good rather than the turning away from an illicit object. Although there is not conflict, there is indeed pain—not at the loss of the transcended creature (for there is no loss, since the movement "beyond" is still always "through" or "in" the creature), but the pain of anxious yearning for the as yet unattained Source of the beautiful.

> As the creatures have given the soul signs of her beloved by revealing to her in themselves a trace of his beauty and excellence, love has increased and, consequently, her pain at his absence has grown. For the more the soul knows God, so much more grows her desire and anguish to see him.
>
> (*Cant.* 6:2)

The total passivity in which creatures are receiving their beauty from God is thus carried over into man's contemplative response: the more he discerns their beauty, the more he sees them as transparently open towards God and is drawn towards that Source. The great spiritual principle of the believer's displacement of the centre of existence from self into God, which is the key to St. John's spiritual life, is also the fundamental law of all creaturely being.

For St. John, therefore, there is a great harmony, or rather an interpenetration, of subjective spiritual life and objective created reality. Within the common sphere of creatureliness the spiritual subject possesses himself in consciousness according to the same law of being. Therefore the true contemplative response is not just a matter of reaching beyond a beautiful "object" conceived in a too extroverted sense; the subjective dimension, the very experience of the beautiful, is bound by the same rigorous law of transcendence. The spiritual life itself is a most beautiful reality, and genuine perceptions of God can be exquisitely so. Nevertheless, as particular experiences, they are simply part of the soul's own life and being, "creaturely" realities themselves, and therefore to be surpassed for God's sake.

Each sight that the soul receives of the Beloved, whether of knowledge or feeling or any other communication, ...making it tedious to be lingering with so little, she thus says: "Surrender yourself now completely".

(*Cant.* 6:4)

Transcendence of the beautiful is thus also essentially a matter of self-transcendence. For that reason, when we suggested that St. John's spirituality might be seen as an aesthetic, we qualified it as being virile and religiously transformed. Beauty is so thoroughly sacramental for him that there is no experience of it which holds him within the confines of this world or of himself. For all his tenderness and compassion, there is no place at all for the slightest religious dilettantism. He thus guides us towards the possession of true Beauty, the beauty of the Beloved, only to the extent that we obey the call to renunciation at the heart of every particular grace.

"...With His Reflection Alone": Creation in Christ.

God's act of creation and the very appearance of the world is signed with the presence of the eternal Son. John of the Cross recognizes the diversity and form running through creation as a harmony played by the Wisdom of God; but he identifies that Wisdom still more closely—"...and doing all this through his Wisdom by which he made them, which is the Word, his only-begotten Son" (*Cant.* 5:1). Now while this Trinitarian and Christological meaning is a normal part of Christian doctrine of Creation, St. John gives it a distinctive quality which reveals the doctrine deeply assimilated into spiritual life. For, just as with the "nothingness" of creation, so, too, this specifically Christian meaning of creation is disclosed *within* his contemplation of nature and is not merely an extrinsic doctrinal gloss upon an "a-Christian" experience of natural contemplation. If creation's passivity under God bears the form of the divine Triune life, and if that passivity is carried over into the soul in contemplation of nature, then that contemplation will also have a real Trinitarian quality.

This special perception of St. John will be more apparent if we notice how he develops his theological source from St. Augustine. For the great African Doctor, the contemplation of nature is a kind dialectic, involving question and answer: "My questioning was my beholding of them, and their answer was their beauty."[4] St. John captures that concise sacramental meaning in his explanatory paraphase of the first part: "As St. Augustine says, the question that the soul puts to the creatures is the mediation that she makes by their means upon the Creator" (*Cant.* 4:1). The original perspective is faithfully preserved: the ultimate finality of man's searching gaze (*intentio mea*) is not the creatures themselves but the Creator ("What do I love when I love Thee?"—St. Augustine). And in both writers the quest for God is directed proximately towards creatures and receives its answer directly from them ("...their answer was their beauty"). Nevertheless, St. John adds his own significant qualification. The loud testimony which creatures make to Augustine is "God made us".[5] Such also is the answer heard by John, but with a clear Trinitarian determination:

> The creatures make answer to the soul, which answer, as St. Augustine also says in the same place, is the testimony they give in themselves concerning the greatness and excellence of God ... and doing all this through his Wisdom through which he created them, which is the Word, his only-begotten Son.
>
> (*Cant.* 5:1)

In fact, Augustine declares no such explicitly Christian answer from the creatures. It would seem to be a particularly vivid element in John's vision of the world. This is not to say that he believes the Trinity can be revealed merely by creation: it is simply that he is listening *in faith* to the witness of creation, a faith which illumines that witness by the fullness of God's

---

[4]"Interrogatio mea intentio mea, et responsio eorum species eorum". *Confessions*, X, 6.

[5]"Et exclamaverunt voce magna: ipse fecit nos". *Ibid.*

self-revelation in the Scriptures. That revelation of Christ is echoed in his listening to the creatures. There is a unity in his experience of Christ and of the world, and so there is nothing extravagant in the creatures speaking to him of the creative Word; even, as we shall see, the Word incarnate in Christ.

The notion of God's creative contemplation is perfected in this theology of the Word. It is not just a question of God in his enigmatic Unity beholding his creation as external to himself, the mystery of his inner life remaining totally remote from creation and relevant only to the super-imposed revealed mystery of redemption. The creation of the world is in vital relationship with the divine generation of the Word, the eternal Image of God's own being.

> According to St. Paul, the Son of God is the brightness of his glory and the figure of his substance (Heb 1:3). It should be known, then, that God gazed upon all things in this image (*figura*) of his Son alone, which was to give them natural being, communicating to them many natural gifts and graces, making them finished and perfect, just as he says in Genesis in these words: 'God saw all the things that he had made and they were very good' (Gen 1:31). To gaze on them as very good was to make them very good in the word, his Son.
>
> (*Cant.* 5:4)

Hans Urs von Balthasar remarks on a certain fruitful ambiguity in this notion of the Son as God's *figura*.[6] It might suggest the Son as the expression of God towards others, "the face of the Father turned towards the world", in the contemplation of which man can come to know the hidden God. This might be a more accurate Scriptural reading of the image, suggested also by John's turning immediately to consider the Incarnation. On the other hand, there is no doubt that in this passage the principal contemplative is not the soul but God himself, who beholds in the Son the perfect figure of himself: in that figure God knows and loves all creatures into being. The theological

---

[6]*The Glory of the Lord*, vol III, Edinburgh, 1986, p 149.

power of this reading is that the Creator's primary intention is not away from Himself towards his works, the Son merely being a consequent 'world-soul' or form of that creation. The meaning of the world is contained *within* the Word, wholly enclosed in the eternal life of the Triune God. Creation's dependence and passivity, then, is not of a helpless, exposed object of detached divine observation, but is nurtured within God's immanent life and thought. Moreover, there is a profound consequence for a theology of contemplation: a most beautiful part of the whole order of creation is the very act of man contemplating that beauty, and that subjective reality of the spiritual life is as much the effect of God's loving contemplation of all things in his Word as is the natural order itself. St. John therefore understands that his own loving perception of creatures is a trace or a living reflection of God's own primal, originating contemplation of the human contemplative in the midst of the world.

Because creation is such a thoroughly theological mystery, so deeply informed by the divine personal activity, there is a real continuity between it and God's saving intervention in the course of the world's history. God passed through the groves of creation "in haste" in his creative work: but "the greater works, in which he showed himself more and in which he had more care, were those of the incarnation of the Word and the mysteries of the Christian faith" (*Cant* 5:3). Creation and redemption are all works (*hechas*), some greater, some less, from the hand of God. There is a unity of divine purpose which binds them together, such that the beauty of creation is not only a reflection of God's creative Word, but also a gleam of the future glory which they are to share in the glorification (the Johannine "lifting up") of the same Word Incarnate. The Incarnation is, *ipso facto,* a cosmic event. It is the trace of Christ which St. John perceives in the loveliness of the world.

> And not only did God communicate to them natural graces and being by gazing on them, as we have said, but also, with only this figure of his Son, he left them clothed with beauty, communicating to them supernatural being; which happened when he became man, exalting him in the beauty of God and, consequently, exalting all creatures in him by

having united himself with the nature of them all in man. For this reason the same Son of God said, 'I, if I be lifted upon from the earth, will draw all things to myself' (Jn 12:32). And thus, in this lifting up of the Incarnation of his Son and of the glory of his resurrection according to the flesh, not only did the Father beautify the creatures partly, but we can say that he left them totally clothed with beauty and dignity.

(Cant. 5:4)

Although the Incarnation is an initiative of God which waits upon man's acceptance of it in faith, there is, nevertheless, some sense in which man, and, through man's corporeality, the whole of creation, cannot but be touched by this gesture of God in which "he united himself with the nature of them all". John is not denying that a strict and proper meaning of transformation by grace depends upon the individual's living faith. He makes it clear that his principal concern is with a union "which is not being wrought continuously, but only when there is produced that likeness that comes from love" (*Asc.* II, 5, 3), a "supernatural" union as distinguished from the "natural" union of God's conserving action. Nevertheless, the very fact of the Incarnation ("which happened when he became man") has transformed the meaning of even the material universe by establishing an entirely new relationship between God and the world, which John describes in a loose sense as "communicating supernatural being".

Thus, simply with the divine-human covenant embodied in the person of Christ (c.f. 2 Cor 1:19f; Heb 10:5-7), the whole of creation has been displaced, 'passively', into a higher realm of meaning by God's redeeming initiative. It is a kind of exigence sown in the nature of all things, which calls upon man to give spiritual expression to it by his surrender of self to God in loving faith (c.f. Rom 8:18ff).

"The Grove and its Beauty in the Serene Night": The Cosmic Dimension of Mystical Union

We have seen that the passivity of the universe under God's creative action passes over to become a function of the soul's spiritual life in contemplation. St. John of the Cross provides us with an account of this meeting of doctrine and life as it is fulfilled in mystical union, where truths hitherto acknowledged in a discursive confession of faith are now apprehended in a new heightened awareness.[7] Among these truths is that of the destiny of the whole creation to share in the glory of the children of God. The soul's sheer createdness is something shared by all other beings, material and spiritual. When grace has completed its purifying and illuminating work, the glorious play of the divine Word appears to reverberate beyond the limitations of the soul's particular being into the whole of creation.

> For this awakening is a movement of the Word in the substance of the soul, of such greatness, dominion and glory and of such intimate sweetness that it seems to the soul that ... all the kingdoms and dominions of the world and all the powers and virtues of heaven are moved. And, not only that; but all the virtues and substances and perfections and graces of all created things shine out and make the same movement together and in unison.... When this great Emperor moves in the soul ... all the spheres seem to be moved.
>
> (*L.F.* 4:4)

For St. John, mystical union, for all that it is achieved in the innermost "substance of the soul", is not individualist and isolating. His reconciliation with God includes the restoration of the divine harmony between God and the whole universe, so much so that his personal mystical union seems to include an anticipated vision of the pleroma.

A great shift in perspective has taken place in this transformation. At the beginning of her quest in the *Spiritual Canticle*, the soul had put the question of God's presence to certain "groves": they were the various orders of creation,

[7]The latter part of the *Spiritual Canticle* treats of the spiritual betrothal (st. 13-21) and spiritual marriage (st. 22-40). The *Living Flame* is almost entirely devoted to a special aspect of spiritual marriage (c.f. Prol, 3); all, that is, except a small section on the passive might of spirit (1:18-26).

wondrously prolific, varied and beautifully ordered (*Cant.* 4f).
Now, in union with the Beloved at the consummation of her
ascent, the image has changed: "by the groves, the soul here
understands God, since he nurtures and gives being to all
creatures, which have their life and root in him" (*Cant.* 39:11).
There is more than mere literary flexibility in this change of
meaning of the groves from the creatures themselves to the
God who contains them. It represents a profound change in
John's perception of creature and Creator. In the earlier way
of meditation he has moved to a joyful love of God the
designer, but only by a movement of renunciation, heading by
faith "through" finite beauty towards its mysterious Source.
Now, after the mutual commitment of love in the spiritual
betrothal, he has come into possession both of God and of the
creation which opened the way to him. There are two complementary modes of that possession. One of them is the
fulfillment of the soul's transcending of all creation to find
God alone—having been left behind, creatures are then re-
discovered transformed "in God":

> the soul knows equally that God, in his own Being, is all
> these things in an infinite and pre-eminent way, so much so
> that it understands them better in his Being than in them-
> selves.
>
> (*L.F.* 4:5)

However, it is not as though this comprehensive transcendent
unity of God's glorious Being obliterates creatures in their
particularity. There is a complementary experience of the
holiness of God "in creatures", in their individual and manifold
existence:

> Insofar as the soul is here united with God, it feels that all
> things are God, as St. John felt when he said: "What was
> made, in him was life" (Jn 1:4). And it must not be thought
> that what the soul is here said to feel is like seeing things in
> the light or creatures in God, but that in that possession it
> feels that all things are God to it.
>
> (*Cant.* 14-15:5)

St. John is able to use such strong expressions of virtual
identity between God and creation, not because he has veered
into pantheism in this mystical experience, but, quite the
contrary, because he is absolutely clear in that experience "that
all these things are distinct from God" (*L.F.* 4:5). (Some of his
well-meaning editors were not at all so secure—a number of
the early manuscripts significantly omit the most challenging
passages). The boldness of his expression is an index of the
power of supraconceptual perception by which he "sees" that
ultimately the whole meaning of any creature is simply its
God-given meaning—"each one exalts God in its own way,
since it has God in itself according to its capacity" (*Cant.*
14-15:27).

Mystical union therefore includes a kind of prophetic discernment of two extreme limits of creation—the complete
integration of all things together and the perfect individuation
of each. Such a radical transformation lies quite beyond the
scope of the intrinsic powers of the universe: it can only be
received as grace, and so it is only in God's transcendent love
that John perceives the resolving of the tension between the
individual and the universal, between delicate intimacy and
cosmic glory. The more he is possessed by the love of God in
the depths of his individual, personal existence, the more he is
able to discern that love working to the limits of creation. His
testimony to this experience is awesome:

> Who could speak fittingly of this intimate point of the
> wound which seems to strike in the centre of the heart of
> the spirit, which is where the fine point of the delight is felt?
> ... The soul feels its ardour to be increasing and growing in
> strength and its love becoming so refined in that ardour,
> that there appear to be in it seas of loving fire which reach
> to the height and depth of the spheres, filling it wholly with
> love. Here it seems to the soul that the whole universe is a
> sea of love in which it is engulfed; it can see no term or
> bound where this love ceases, feeling within itself, as we
> have said, the living point and centre of love.
>
> (*L.F.* 2:10)

Here then is a consummation of the Gospel Way which must
be utterly beyond all human guessing. That Way is to resign

freely and wholly all the intentions of one's life into God, to
displace the entire meaning of one's own existence and that of
all other beings into the divine Word, at once consuming and
sustaining. But to be thus given over into Love is to dwell at
the creative source and final meaning of all things, and so to
find oneself restored to the very centre of one's own personal
being and to the living heart of the whole world. Even though
St. John resorts to the traditional but somewhat ambiguous
image of the drop lost in the ocean—modified by his particular
ardour into an ocean of fire—this union is patently no falling
away of individuality into an amorphous One. The principle
of union, the Holy Spirit, being completely transcendent,
respects the uniqueness of all that it embraces—and not merely
respects it, but, granted the simultaneous condition of perfect
selflessness, enhances it in perfect self-possession, "in the
farthest point attained by its own substance, virtue, and power"
(*L.F.* 1:14).

Finally, certain features of the spiritual life which are commonly regarded as merely subjective techniques of receptivity,
are elevated by St. John into a theological and cosmic context.
Silence and solitude are not just self-imposed conditions for
individual perfection, as though they were ascetic means to be
discarded at the end of the ascent. John sees them as abiding
values of spiritual existence, since they are qualities not only of
God's revealing himself in the economy of salvation, but also
of his immanent Trinitarian life:

> One word spoke the Father, which was his Son, and he is
> speaking it always in eternal silence, and in silence it must
> be heard by the soul.
>
> (*Sayings* 98)

If perfection is something essentially received, a word of God
heard, so silence is the pure ambience of that receptivity. Far
from being the hollow absence of communion, its authentic
form is the perfect attentiveness which alone can discern the
Word of God, both in his immediate relationship with the soul
and in the harmony of all creation. That harmony of creation
is a music which God plays to his Bride-soul, a "silent" music,
because "it is a tranquil and quiet intelligence, without noise of

voices, and in it are enjoyed both the sweetness of the music and the quiet of silence" (*Cant.* 14-15:25). Silence is the unfailing complement of God's universal harmony, the pure region undisturbed by the disparate "voices" of creatures heard in isolation from God. St. John's care for the ascetic discipline of silence in the monastery is therefore a love of the sacramental form of that silent music in the life of the community. The lives of the brethen together are to form a microcosm of that harmony, neither profaned by empty chatter not silenced in the tomb of dead, rigorist observance. Wherever he was prior, the house was notably quiet and happy. Authentic solitude is likewise no desolate isolation.

> For although that music is silent to the senses and natural powers, it is a most sonorous solitude to the spiritual powers.
>
> (*Cant.* 14-15:26)

In the dark renunciation of contemplative faith, John has made himself "remote" from particular creatures in their "natural" or "outward" mode of existence—that is, in the shell of mere appearance by which they are divorced from their true place in God.

Solitude of one kind or another is therefore an inescapable condition of human and spiritual life:

> In solitude she lived,
> and in solitude now has built her nest,
> and in solitude there guides her
> solely her Beloved,
> who also in solitude was wounded by love.
>
> (*Cant.* 35)

It begins as a figure of alienation. Far from the Beloved in its self-centred grasping, the soul's every attempt to contrive or force companionship carries its own seed of inevitable disappointment—"before it finds God, everything causes it a greater solitude" (*Cant.* 35:3). But if, through love, that grasping is reversed to willing dispossession, then what was merely a brutal and destructive fact of alienation is experienced in a new, creative meaning as the way to the Beloved. The "nest" which the soul has built in solitude is indeed a resting place and a comfort, but it is the comfort of the happy recognition that ultimately every need of companionship is fulfilled in God. It is therefore a figure of simultaneous detachment and fulfillment—willingness to be without all things for the sake of the Beloved, and a dwelling-place in God where all desires and potentialities are fulfilled (*Cant.* 35:4). It is a way of simultaneous action and passivity—fundamentally, a peace in loving communion which can only be "discovered" (*hallar*) or received as the Beloved's free gift of himself, but which also cannot be received without the soul's "working" (*ejercitar*), "seeking" (*procurar*) with dedicated striving. Indeed, the dispossession of self for God's sake, so far from leaving an impotent shell of a person, has such power that St. John speaks of it daringly as bearing upon God with a reciprocal force of love:

> For, besides the Spouse greatly loving the solitude of the soul, he is much more wounded with love of her in that she has desired to remain alone, far from all things, since she was wounded with love for him.
>
> (*Cant.* 35:7)

The way to union has come full circle. It was God's transcendence, experienced in the destructive context of selfish living, which formed the solitude of alienation at the beginning. But that transcendence was a relentless summons to an ever more perfect renunciation of creatures, including even the soul's own being and her own appropriated experiences of God. And yet it is this faithfulness to that divine transcendence, this obedience to that summons, which wounds and conquers the heart of God and gains his loving communion. And, as we have seen, that communion with God restores authentic communion with all things "in God": in a cosmic harmony they are given back to man "in their truth" (*Sayings,* 48).

Like the silence, so the solitude of St. John's Carmelite life is sacramental of this wider spiritual universe. By temperament he seems to have lacked the easy conviviality of St. Teresa, and yet there is ample testimony from those who lived with him to his unstinting sensitive care and his unfeigned, simple affection. At the same time, that love was conditioned by a deep respect and discretion which shunned any intrusive or contrived camaraderie. Out of his own experience of knowing the intimacy of God's unique love for him, he could entrust his brethren into that same sphere of solitary communion, knowing that they would be no less tenderly and generously met by God and that in this shared charism of seclusion they were coming together in a hidden communion in the Spirit.

To conclude: a theology of Creation provides the proper foundation for understanding and reconciling two most fundamental features of St. John of the Cross' spiritual life—his uncompromising demand for renunciation and his manifest overflowing joy in created goodness and beauty. All things are continuously proceeding from the generous love of God. Creating with love by his Word, and recreating through the Incarnation of the Word and the gift of the Spirit of love, God is always the first transcendent Giver. John therefore knows himself to be simply placed, prior to any response of his own, in a fundamental condition of passivity, receiving the world around him and even his own life and existence. And because of that constant total dependence, the very gift of being is itself a summons back to union with God, a summons fully articulated and made effective in Jesus Christ. John's spirituality may therefore be seen as an ever deeper realization in himself of the mystery of universal gravitation of all meaning into God. If all created things and his own life are bestowed upon him, it is so that they should be "left behind" in the sense of becoming transparent to the presence of the Giver; or, better, that they should impel him with their own powerful stream of self-displacement towards the divine centre.

3

Shades of Night

How well I know the fountain brimming, flowing,
Although it is the night.

Darkness and light play in a constant lively pattern in the life of St. John. The air of the high plateau of his native Castile has a special clarity which gives brilliance to light and a sharp black edge to shadow and night, and these seem to have been bred into his sensibility and marked his faith. There are many witnesses to his great love of the night. He would often go out into it to pray, sometimes with a companion, frequently alone— under the trees, near the river among the crags, open to the stars. "More lovely than the dawn", it was the natural ambience of his communion with God.

He found that communion also in the bleak shadow of a prison cell. During the nine months of hidden captivity in Toledo, when some authorities were trying to stamp out the Discalced Reform, he was confined in a small kind of internal store room, a cavity in a wall about six feet by ten. It was scarcely lit by a small window, high in the wall, opening into another room. Until, after several months, he was given a small lamp by a kindly gaoler, he had to stand on a small stool to pray from his breviary so as to win just enough light for the text. In the deeper shadow of the floor he was left only with his own communion of faith—out of which he composed the first loving stanzas of the *Spiritual Canticle* and the haunting faith-music of "*Aunque es la noche,* Although it is the night".

In a white-painted house only a short distance away, El Greco was painting the Christian mysteries with an unmatched dynamism of shadow and unearthly light, a light which does not bathe the scene but breaks out from within it, either from the person of Jesus or from the mysterious divine presence lying close behind the physical forms. All these things suggest a natural visible counterpart to St. John's doctrine of the Dark Night of the soul.

A cursory acquaintance with St. John's writings will arm the reader with some notions, such as "the night of spirit", "the passive night of sense", etc., which have become common currency in Western[6]mystical theology and which are taken to indicate certain "stages" in the spiritual life. Unfortunately, the very poetic and evocative nature of these terms has sometimes led to a facile and slack usage in later writings—a sad irony when on considers just how finely discerning was St. John's experiential knowledge which gave rise to this classic imagery. Therefore it might be helpful to offer a kind of preliminary chart by which to locate the different "nights", or phases of the night of faith, through which the soul passes on its way to union with God.

St. John builds his analysis on two pairs of terms, 'sense' and 'spirit', 'active' and 'passive'. By combining these pairs he arrives at a four-fold division:

> The first night of purgation is of the sensitive part of the soul ... which will be treated in the first part of this book [*Asc.* I]. And the second is of the spiritual part, ... and of this we shall treat likewise in second and third part [*Asc.* II and III] with regard to the active dimension; and, with regard to the passive, this will be treated in the fourth part [*D.N.* I and II].

For all the panoply of supposed clear Scholastic analysis, it is obvious that St. John himself is not wiithout blame for the later confusion, and the complexity is compounded by his editors' practice of publishing the *Dark Night* as a separate treatise rather than as the "fourth part" of a single work. Nevertheless, in the light of several other methodological passages[1] we can take the following sequence with some certainty to be St. John's ultimate intention: active night of sense (*Asc* I), active night of spirit (*Asc.* II and III), passive night of sense (*D.N.* I), passive night of spirit (D.N. II).

Such is the formal, logical pattern: as such, it has an impressive coherence and completeness. However, the most important question remains—what foundation is there in actual spiritual living, in the enormous complexity and variability of a person's experience of prayer, for this clear theoretic four-fold division? The conceptual framework is meant to enhance the meaning of all the find threads which makes up the robe of an individual's actual life with God, not to obliterate them in a neat, abstract system. In his own lifetime St. John was revered and loved for his conversations of spiritual direction, in which elements of his penitent's experience which were hitherto opaque, burdensome, apparently self-enclosing and futile were suddenly rendered luminous and found their "place" as true steps, though perhaps still painful and dark, on the journey with Christ to God. His written works must serve that purpose for us. And so we have to recognize that St. John's ordered teatment of the nights does not mean that they must simply be four consecutive phases in the soul's spiritual evolution. Every reference to the "night of spirit" need not mean some arcane and rare mystical purification, nor is every "passive purification" a sublime experience of God's work in the soul.

The Active Night of Sense

In the different modes of purification and illumination, the active night of sense has a certain foundational role and will usually come first. "The point from which the soul goes forth" (*Asc.* I, 2, 1) on its spiritual progress should be marked by resolve for an active programme of ascesis. It refers specifically not to a mode of prayer, but to a virtuous discipline of life of which the vigour of self-commitment to God is necessary for a deeper communion of prayer. In the language of the ancient

[1] *Asc.* I, 13, 1; *Asc.* II, 2, 2f; *D.N.* I, 8, 1f.

monastic tradition of John Cassian and the Desert Fathers, it is the "practical" (praktikē) knowledge in the improvement of morals and correction of faults which is the essential ground for contemplative (theoretikē) knowledge of the divine mysteries.[2] The active night of sense, then, is the dusk that preludes the sheer darkness of contemplative faith (*Asc.* I, 2, 5). It means not only the correction of obvious habits of sin, but also the willing restraint of sensuous satisfactions which in themselves may be morally quite legitimate but which can all too easily trap the soul in complacent routine. Thus it is a "night" in virtue of being a privation of ordinary pleasures and consolations. It is "active" inasmuch as one deliberately undertakes such privation—and indeed emphatically so, to judge by St. John's characteristically vehement expressions of the soul "denying", "rejecting", "thrusting away from itself" the pleasures of the senses (*Asc.* I, 3, 2; passim). And, finally, it is a voluntary restraint of the "senses". This last term must be taken in a somewhat wider meaning than the strict metaphysical distinction between sense and spirit. It refers rather to all the good things of this world and of natural human living.

And here, of course, it is of the utmost importance to recall all that we have said concerning the true ascetical meaning of "mortification of the desires and denial of pleasures in all things" (*Asc.* I, 4, 1). It does not aim at insensibility—witness the exquisite harmonies of St. John's own lyric poetry which gives expression to this very night of sense—but rather at liberating the soul from the dark prison of self-centred gratification, a freedom to choose the true good.

St. John speaks of a certain order or sequence between this ascetic active night of sense and the further nights of contemplative prayer. The false darkness of unmortified desire must give way before the pure and simple light of God in contemplation. He is as uncompromising in his doctrine as is the Gospel. St. John the Evangelist's great spiritual polarities of light and darkness and the witness of Paul the Apostle[3] are invoked to confirm this pattern of spiritual growth: "the light

[2] Cassian, *Cons.* XIV, 1-3.

[3] Jn 1:5; 2 Cor 6:14; *Asc.* loc. cit.

of divine union cannot dwell in the soul if these affections are not first made to flee away from it" (*Asc.* I, 4, 2). Nevertheless, there are very important qualifications to be made concerning this sequence of ascetical and contemplative nights. St. Teresa herself, with her inimitable irony and incisive common sense, rose in playful protest against John's radical, uncompromising demands in his commentary on the words "Seek thyself in me". She answers:

> It would be a bad business for us if we could not seek God until we were dead to the world. Neither the Magdalen, nor the woman of Samaria, nor the Canaanite woman was dead to the world when she found him.... God deliver me from people who are so spiritual that they want to turn everything into perfect contemplation, come what may. At the same time we are grateful for having been given so good an explanation of what we had not asked about.
>
> (*Judgement*)

God's readiness to grant particular gifts of prayer, and especially of transient extraordinary phenomena, is not simply proportionate to the recipient's achieved moral condition. It may well happen that a person experiences certain genuine gifts of prayer of an elevated kind while not yet having attained that habitual spiritual maturity which is the "normal" context for such gifts. St. John himself was well aware of the total gratuitousness of all God's supernatural gifts: the divine loving interventions transcend and put to confusion all the human calculation of a too neat "system" of spiritual theology.

> Not that it is always necessary for God to observe this order [of progressive, well-regulated graces] and to cause the soul to advance exactly in this way from the first step to the last; sometimes he allows the soul to attain one stage and not another, or leads it from the more interior to the less, or effects two stages of progress together. This happens when God sees it to be fitting for the soul or when he desires to grant it his favours in this way.
>
> (*Asc.* II, 17, 4)

Speculative theology can discern a genuine order in spiritual growth—there are certain qualities of soul which are the necessary condition for entering into a relationship of personal intimacy with God. But God always has the initiative, and his very intervention, which is experienced as a mystical passivity, can itself create the condition of soul appropriate for the new mode of relationship. The requisite capacity for receiving passive mystical graces is not simply the fruit of active ascesis. Such graces cannot be earned, and in fact, to the mystic himself, the gift of prayer will always seem to be vastly disproportionate to his poor preparation or "merits". True, if it is a genuine spiritual growth then the person must be freely consenting: the mystic is no spiritual automaton. But that free consent is deeply interwoven with the work of grace, and while there may be a certain logical priority of the active personal consent by which the gift of God's love is accepted, in actual experience it is simultaneous with the grace strengthening the will to assent and with the perceived passive mystical fruition. For God is wholly transcendent, and although the order of spiritual growth has its necessary conditions, God is not subject to a fixed pattern. He freely and wisely shapes that growth in a living, creative way, formed in each individual according to his own unique design for that person—"...as he sees fit, ... when he so desires"(*loc. cit.*). The notion that active penitential discipline must precede the passive experience of contemplation is a generalization from the more frequently occuring pattern of spiritual growth; it is not a law which determines every case.

St. John gives another reason why the active night of sense marks the beginning of spiritual growth: it "belongs to the lower part of man, which is the sensuous and, consequently, the more exterior" (*Asc.* II, 2, 2). In a spirituality which conceives growth as a progressive interiorization, with transforming grace penetrating toward the deepest centre of the soul (*L.F.* 1:9-14), the locus of the initial stages will be the more exterior domain of sense.[4]

---

[4]This will be true at least as regards conscious awareness. St John's interiorization is to a significant extent, though by no means exclusively, an awakening of the inner depths of the person to conscious awareness in God's presence. He certainly does not reduce the reality of grace to be merely coextensive with this inner experience. Before

Once again we must add an important qualification. For all that deliberate bodily discipline and penance is a kind of preparation for the more spiritual gifts, it is never wholly transcended. The "exterior" region of physical asceticism is not supplanted by the "interior" gifts of contemplation. There will indeed be change in the forms of asceticism: contemplative gifts of illuminating self-knowledge will reveal faults hitherto concealed, and ascetic activity should become more discerning and sensitive, aiming at the root causes of sin. But some kind of exterior physical ascesis will always have a role in the spiritual life, no matter how advanced and interior, if for no other reason than the fact of the never-ceasing role of the senses in all human life and the tenacious weaknesses and disorders of that sensitivity inherited through original sin: "to take away these [natural desires and their disorder]—that is, to mortify them wholly in this life—is impossible" (*Asc.* I, 11, 2). St. John professes this sober fact not with dismay nor with recoil from the physical quality of human existence. On the contrary, his insistence on the correction and purification of the senses reveals an abiding care for that dimension of human and Christian life. Spiritual progress for St. John is not a matter of progressive disembodiment. Unlike numerous 'spiritual' sects, such as the Alumbrados of his own day, his "perfect soul" never leaves behind the desire and reverence for full human integrity.

The Active Night of Spirit
and Passive Night of Sense

St. John considers the next phase of spiritual growth under the heading of "the active night of spirit" (*Asc.* II & III). However, in the concrete reality of a person's spiritual life there is no real chronological sequence between this and "the passive night of sense" which he treats in Book I of the *Dark*

---

the web of this mortal life is broken, the profoundest works of God's grace must be hidden from our weak, untransfigured sight. Even the mystic has only intimations, not clear and essential vision, of immortality.

Night. The distinction between these two nights is genuine enough, but it is mainly a theoretical one in which activity and passivity signify two aspects of the one experience.

What, then, is that experience designated by this two-fold night? We can most clearly grasp its nature if, reversing St. John's order of discussion, we consider it first under the aspect of the passive night of sense.[5] The kind of prayer which characterized the beginnings of the ascent is that of active, discursive meditation. St. John, in fact, has little to say about it: it is something that he simply presumes will be present in the life of anyone who is seeking God with any serious intent. He does not envisage it as being at all problematic, and so he alludes to it only in passing, as that which is to be transcended by modes of higher, contemplative, prayer—

> meditation, a discursive action wrought by means of images, forms and figures that are fashioned by the [interior] senses, as when we imagine Christ crucified, or bound to the column, or at another of the stations.
>
> (*Asc.* II, 12, 3)

It is the pattern of prayer most commonly associated now with the *Spiritual Exercises* of St. Ignatius, although we must understand it to include every kind of discursive prayer— spontaneous simple conversation with God, set formulae of verbal prayer, reflective reading of the Scriptures as a prayerful hearing the word of God, etc.[6]

---

[5]St John himself follows an ascending hierarchy: man's activity of spirit (*Asc* II and III) is a less sublime aspect than his passivity (*D.N.* I) because this latter is really his being receptive to a higher, divine activity.

[6]That St John so easily presumes this simple prayerful access to God to be present in "beginners" is an index of the massive shift in religious culture from sixteenth-century Spain to the present ethos of the Western world. Whatever might have been the moral and spiritual failure in a person's life at that time, and granted the real harbingers of modern secularism in some strands of the genius of Renaissance humanism, still the fundamental parameters of a Christian world-view held good for the vast majority of people. God was a personal reality who might indeed be loved or disobeyed or even forgotten for a time, but without whom a whole view of the world and one's personal life was scarcely conceivable. Speaking to him came more naturally; his Incarnation into their world was accepted as simple fact. Thus, El Greco, painting in his house in Toledo only a short distance from St. John in his prison cell, dissolved

The second phase is recognized in contradistinction to this, by a new and strange inability to make such meditation. All the "consolations of sense" which had seemed to be such intrinsic and inevitable elements of prayer—the peace and joy of experiencing simple conversation with God as a real communication of one's mind and heart, the affective involvement in the mysteries of the life of Christ, the wonder and awe and love in entering into God's revelation of himself in the Scriptures—all of this gives way to an ambient of constraint, darkness and aridity.

> Just as they believe that the sun of divine favour is shining most brightly upon them, God turns all this light of theirs into darkness. . . . They do not know where to go with their sensible imagination and meditation; for they cannot advance a step in meditation as they used to do, their inward senses being submerged in this night.
>
> (*D.N.* I, 8, 3)

This is not a matter of deliberately choosing to simplify the operations of the mind in order to elicit a still, "contemplative" ethos. For St. John, the initiative for authentic contemplation belongs to God, not to the soul. And this desolation or "night of sense" in prayer is distinctly "passive", not something that one contrives but which one must undergo, even "suffer". Indeed, this condition is itself one of the essential "signs" for discerning whether God is intervening with contemplative grace: the soul is simply unable to meditate as before, "however much it may of itself endeavour to do so" (*D.N.* I, 9, 8). Contrariwise, for as long as one is able to draw nourishment and relish from discursive prayer, one would do wrong not to avail of it (*Asc.* II, 13, 2; 15, 1f).

It should be noted that these descriptions of the passive night of sense are found not only in their 'proper' place, Book I of the *Dark Night*, but also in Book II of the *Ascent,* that is,

---

the forms and horizons of this world so that they became immediately present to the mystical light and darkness of heaven. A generation later, Velasquez would render an old Spanish woman and a girl in a kitchen with unmatched sensuous immediacy—and, in the next room, Jesus with Martha and Mary.

in the discussion of the active night of spirit. This is because, as we have already said, these two nights are, in fact, two facets of the one actual experience.

And so, simultaneously with this passive deprivation of "sense" activity, there is to be exercised a new activity of the spirit. This is the vital heart of Christian prayer, that which St. John calls, in a very specific sense, "faith". Not that the earlier way of meditation could possibly be made without faith in its normal and proper sense, but a new and more pure mode of the exercise of faith in prayer becomes possible only as the night of sense subdues idea and image which are, as it were, the particular forms or embodiments of the vital act of believing:

> it consists not in labouring with the imagination, but in setting the soul at rest and allowing to remain in its quiet and repose, which is more spiritual. For the farther the soul progresses in spirituality, the more it ceases from the operation of the faculties in particular acts, since it becomes more and more occupied in one act that is general and pure.
>
> (*Asc.* II, 12, 6)

And so this night of faith is "active" in a specific and peculiar way. It certainly has nothing of busyness about it. It does not move from point to point as in discursive reflection; rather, this act of pure believing has a *singleness* ("one act") which involves a certain stillness and repose, a very simple "being present" to God. And it is also most definitely an *act,* vital and alert, "an attentiveness (*atencion*) and a knowledge, general and loving" (*Asc.* II, 13, 4). It is as though all the vital resources of consciousness which are usually expressed in, and in some way dissipated by, discursive thinking, are here concentrated, "changed into the substance of loving knowledge" (*Asc,* II, 14, 2). It is a certain loving gaze into the dark reaches of faith where God is known to dwell, an activity which, for all its simplicity and its "confused and general" nature, is something which the person can discern and faithfully maintain, sustained by the now considerable grace of God. It is a condition of strong, sensitive spiritual attunement to the divine mystery.

This night of faith is also active in another, negative, sense. For in freely committing oneself in prayer to this new mode of attentiveness, one is also deliberately refraining from the pursuit of previous sensible consolations. Such consolations indeed are no longer simply available at will; nevertheless, there may well be an abiding taste and nostalgia for such religious consolation, and these lingering desires must now be resolutely renounced. It is a new kind of spiritual ascesis, a free ("active") acceptance of the inner austerity of prayer which God has initiated.

This simple dark gaze of contemplative faith is itself another of the signs that St. John requires to authenticate the movement into a profounder mode of prayer (*Asc.* II, 13, 4 & 5). Without it, the aridity and distaste for things spiritual and mundane would be no more than some physical or emotional malaise ("some kind of humour in the brain or heart"), and the resulting "peace" nothing more than a natural psychic languor. Hence, the real "God-intention" of this simple spiritual act is absolutely crucial. Nevertheless, St. John also allows that, at least in its initial form, this purer attentiveness of faith may be very difficult to discern. It may in fact be operative in a person, but, because of his unfamiliarity with this new region of consciousness which, as it were, underlies the usual patterns of imaginative and reflective awareness, his predominant self-awareness may have the form merely of the passive night of sense, that is, of darkness, aridity, constraint, while he has not as yet recognized and appropriated in himself the simple, loving attentiveness to the divine mystery in prayer. It is especially to facilitate such discoveries of new regions of consciousness that St. John is writing his treatises, and to support and encourage his spiritual children in those stressful times when the new maturity has not yet emerged. Thus there is a tender patience and gentleness in his direction, reverently giving place to the times and rhythms of God's work in each person. The perseverance he calls for here is not an activist attempt to force some contemplative phenomenon, but a more sensitive and discerning 'let it emerge';

> But the more accustomed the soul grows to this [simple act of contemplative faith], by allowing itself to rest, the more it

will grow therein and the more conscious it will become of
that loving general knowledge of God.

(Asc. II, 13, 7)

He anticipates the anxieties and scruples that can assail people
at such times—"that they are wasting their time, and that it
would be well for them to do something else" *(D.N.* I, 10,
5)—and answers comfortingly that it is quite sufficient, in fact
it is a sign of true fidelity, simply "to persevere in patience", to
trust in the faithfulness of God, "contenting themselves with
merely a peaceful and loving attentiveness towards God, in
being without anxiety, and to perceive him *(D.N.* I, 10, 4).

While it can happen, then, that the conscious experience of
the simple, dark act of faith can thus be delayed somewhat
after the initial experience of the passive night of sense, the
contrary sequence is also possible. Hitherto we have considered
the simple gaze of contemplative faith as an activity which can
be deliberately invoked and held, something which lies within
the soul's own power and competence. Such activity, of course,
would be not at all possible without the intervention of God
both in binding the discursive activity and in infusing the very
gift of faith, but this latter gift is commonly not experienced as
an irruption of God into one's experience. As in any kind of
prayer, the ultimate initiative always belongs to God, but this
grace is largely hidden below the threshold of consciousness.
However, in this further grace of contemplation, the "one act,
general and pure", is now *experienced* as *given* passively. The
divine movement which was previously a subliminal ontological reality, now wells up to become part of the person's
conscious awareness in prayer. Quite perceptibly the movement of prayer now originates from the more interior realms
of spirit, not so much by free self-movement as by another
who indwells the soul and who catches up the soul's natural
energies of loving into His own more powerful current of love
surging from within. The Greek tradition speaks of a "synergy".
These are the forms of contemplative prayer which are more
vividly described by St. Teresa under the headings of passive
recollection or Prayer of Quiet (c.f. IV *Mansions*). With unmatched discernment in these matters, she speaks boldly of the
captivation of love:

The will alone is occupied, in such a way that, without knowing how, it becomes captive. It allows itself to be imprisioned by God, as one who well knows itself to be the captive of him whom it loves. Oh, my Jesus and Lord, how much thy love now means to us! It binds our own love so straitly that at that moment it leaves us no freedom to love anything but thee.

(*Life,* ch 14)

St. John's gift of discernment pertains much more to the dark, "negative" or apophatic modes of contemplation rather than to such positive illuminating graces. Nevertheless, he does give some suggestion of these latter forms even in this early stage of contemplation: the spiritual joy of God's intervention "*is communicated to them* in much greater abundance than before, *overflowing into their senses*" (*D.N.* II, 1, 2, italics added). Here is a strange reversal of the natural order of perception, by which, according to the traditional Aristotelian-Scholastic axiom "non in intellectu, quod non prius in sensu"—nothing is present in the intellect which has not first been present to the senses. Now, however, by this contemplative grace, the movement of prayer originates quite perceptibly from the more interior realms of the spirit, the still hidden regions of divine indwelling, its effects spreading outwards to the senses.

The Passive Night of Spirit

The fourth category, or third principal phase of purification, is the passive night of spirit (*D.N.* II). Its ultimate place in the sequence of purifying nights is both ontological (spirit requiring a more profound purification than sense, and passive purification being a more advanced mode than active), and also chronological. For with this night we are in the sphere of the strictly and unambiguously mystical. Unlike the phase of the active night of spirit/passive night of sense "which is common and comes to many", the passive night of spirit "is the portion of very few" (*D.N.* I, 8, 1). Unlike the first night of contemplation, which often comes upon people "before no great time passes" if they apply themselves to spiritual discipline and regular prayer, the final passive purification is experienced by the few who attain it at all only after "a long time, even years" of faithful correspondence with the contemplative grace of "proficients" (*D.N.* I, 8, 4).

Can we give any indication of the nature of the experience denoted by this heading? St. John himself denies the possibility of adequately describing these dark mysteries (*D.N.* II, 4, 2). As with all things properly mystical, there is here a certain immediacy of spiritual encounter with God, such that not only does the Beloved transcend all human thought, but the locus of this encounter in the human subject is the "substance of the soul" (*D.N.* II, 6, 5; 13, 3), a region of spiritual being which is always anterior to conceptual and reflective consciousness and so defies all utterance.

Nevertheless, it can be indicated indirectly, and St. John does this in two ways. Firstly, there is the allusive power of his poetry and image-laden prose: the sweet and haunting beauty of the 'Noche oscura' song itself declares that there is always that much more which cannot be spoken, and in chapters five to thirteen especially of his commentary he draws upon eloquent passages of Job, Lamentations and the dark Psalms of affliction to compose from them a kind of deep tragic adagio. But in order that the meaning should be more than simply aesthetic and the encounter identified surely as encounter with God, this passive night of spirit is also understood conceptually, within the whole context of spiritual growth, by means of negative theology. And so, just as we most conveniently located the passive night of sense in contradistinction from an earlier phase, namely as the deprivation of ordinary forms of discursive meditation, so the passive night of spirit is also a more radical negation or dispossession. Through a growing proficiency in the dark and loving gaze of faith ("active night of spirit"), the soul had already become more and more capable of relishing "in its spirit the most serene and loving contemplation and spiritual sweetness" (*D.N.* II, 1, 1). More and more has it generously invested the whole of its spiritual resources into this mature single intention of soul, the intention of pure faith, which it knows experientially to be "the proximate and proportionate means of union with God" and which is itself an obscure but direct communion with the Beloved

(*Asc.* II, 9, 4). It is a region of genuine spiritual abundance. But now, just as previously the ability for discursive meditation was taken from it, so, in a far more awesome reversal, the gift of this most precious communion in contemplative faith seems to be annihilated:

> God has set a cloud before it through which its prayer cannot pass.
>
> (*D.N.* II, 8, 1)

Not only is the outer, sensible dimension of the house of prayer stilled, "put to sleep", but the very spring of inner spiritual vitality seems to have been sealed.

This, then is an experience of quite terrible suffering. There is the crushing sense of powerlessness and seeming futility, commensurate with the previous climate in which all the powers of spiritual awareness had really flourished to an extraordinary degree. Sensitivity and quickening of spirit have given way to the suffocating constraint of Jonah in the belly of the whale: "the waters have enclosed me, even to the soul, the deep has shut me in, the ocean has covered my head; I went down to the roots of the mountains, the bars of the earth have shut me in for ever" (Jon 2:5f; *D.N.* II, 6, 3). Moreover, the night which was soft and beautiful with contemplative intimations of God's goodness and holiness has now become the terrible blackness of the awareness of sin:

> And when the soul suffers the direct assault of this divine light, its pain, which results from its impurity, is immense; because, when this pure light assails the soul in order to expel its impurity, the soul feels itself to be so impure and miserable that it believes God to be against it, and thinks that it has set itself up against God.... For, by means of this pure light, the soul now sees its impurity clearly (though darkly), and knows clearly that it is unworthy of God or of any creature.
>
> (*D.N.* II, 5, 5)

It is of utmost importance to recognize that this is a spiritual realism and not a pyschological sickness. St. John is here speaking of a true perception of one's spiritual condition; it is utterly different from the neurosis of "a poor self-image" diagnosed by the psychologist. This latter is a false view of oneself, distorted by inordinate emotional factors, whereas the dark night of spirit is a true experimental knowledge of one's real, radical lack of the spiritual integrity which is proper to a creature made in the image of God. If sin is a profanation of that inestimably holy image, the affliction of the dark night is an immediate confrontation with that profanation. Not that one undergoing this darkness is 'a great sinner' in the common judgement of men; indeed, it is an awareness that belongs only to one who is exceptionally close in mind and heart to the pure light of God, and his self-judgement will usually seem to be exaggerated and unrealistic to those who do not share that depth of divine illumination. But, as is obvious in the passage just quoted and in many others, John declares quite simply and without any demur that the soul perceives its real impurity and unworthiness of God. He can allow the fierce force of that truth because he knows and shares in the even greater truth of God's loving mercy.

On the other hand, there is a certain kind of blindness involved here, not culpable, but due precisely to the proximity and intensity of the divine light. While the soul has a true perception of its unlikeness to God, the true nature of God's loving intention is hidden from it.

> For this reason Saint Dionysius [the Areopagite] and other mystical theologians call this infused contemplation a ray of darkness—that is to say, for the soul that is not enlightened and purged—for the natural strength of the intellect is transcended and overwhelmed by its great supernatural light.
>
> (*D.N.* II, 5, 3)

The very intensity of God's self-giving is more than the soul is able to bear, because of both its natural creaturely limitation and its debility through sin. Of course, that divine self-giving, whether expressed under the figure of light or of fire, is the very essence of love: as John emphasizes in his later account in the *Living Flame*, it is the Holy Spirit, the very same fire of divine love here purifying the soul so painfully which, when that purification is complete, glorifies it in a total harmony of divine-human love. (*L.F.* 1:15-21; c.f. also *D.N.* II, 10). But here, God's loving intention is lost to view. The soul is conscious only of its unlikeness to God, and so "it believes God to be against it, and it thinks that it has set itself up against God" (II, 5, 5); "it appears clear to the soul that God has abandoned it and, in his abhorrence of it, has flung it into darkness"(II, 6, 2); "not able to believe that God loves it, nor that there is or will ever be reason why he should do so"(II, 7, 7).

The inevitable corollary to this awareness of sin is a great sense of loneliness and isolation. The soul feels alienated not only from the love of God but also, because it arises out of a perception of one's seemingly manifest disfigurement of sin, from all one's friends and from the whole of creation. How could anyone love this wretchedness and failure? Like Job, Jeremiah of the *Lamentations,* or the Psalmist in his afflictions, one feels himself to be a blight on the earth, one belongs nowhere. Of the many passages of great pathos in *Dark Night* II, one stands out particularly as an account of St. John's own experience—not just as one who has undergone the darkness himself but as a loving friend and spiritual counsellor standing by the afflicted:

> . . .[the soul] suffers great pain and grief, since there is added to all this (because of the solitude and abandonment caused in it by the dark night) the fact that it finds no consolation or support in any instruction nor in a spiritual master. For although in many ways its director may show it good reason for being comforted because of the blessings which are contained in these afflictions, it cannot believe him. For it is so greatly absorbed and immersed in the realization of those evils in which it sees its own miseries so clearly, that it thinks that, as its director does not observe what it sees and feels, he is speaking in this way because he does not understand it; and so, instead of comfort, it receives rather fresh affliction since it believes that its director's advice contains no remedy for its troubles.

> (*D.N.* II, 7, 3)

Not even the loving care and profound understanding of St. John of the Cross can dispel that darkness. Nor, in a sense, would he wish to. He can only wait until God has done his work in the purifying darkness before the suffering companion is restored to the happiness of shared, trusting, loving understanding. In the meantime, all he expects to do is to keep faith with the afflicted and, by his own patience, compassion and hope in Christ, to sustain his companion's hope almost vicariously in the midst of it all.

It is this sense of being utterly bereft of God and of all friends which is the essence of the affliction of the passive night of spirit. It is what induces John to liken it to hell (II, 6, 2; 6, 6) or to purgatory (II, 7, 7) or, rather, not merely to liken but to identify it with that experience of God-forsakenness. Such a radical spiritual condition is more commonly realized only in death, but as the spirit becomes so refined that the grace-enhanced light of consciousness can reach back into the springs of personhood—"the roots of the spirit" (II, 2, 1) or "spiritual substance" (II, 6, 1, 85)—then such an experience may be undergone by the saints even in this life.

Two important comments must be made to ensure a true understanding of this bold and, for some, this scandalous notion. Firstly, this afflictive darkness is in truth a night *of faith*—not a diminishment, but a deepening of faith, hope and love to an heroic degree. For those who do not sufficiently distinguish the different levels of spiritual existence and experience, this assertion will seem to be contradicted by John's fiercest passages of desolation—"feeling itself to be without God, and castigated, cast out and unworthy of him, and that he is angry; ... and more, for it seems to the soul that it will be thus with it for ever" (II, 6, 2). Even for such a renowned theologian as the Russian Orthodox Vladimir Lossky, such a passage concerning the mystical night can suggest only the sin of, or at best, the temptation to, *acedia,* "a sadness which ends in despair, the greatest sin, the beginning of eternal death".[7] St.

---

[7]*In the Image and Likeness of God,* S.V.S. Press, 1974, p 59, n 36. In this same note Lossky maintains that "the 'mystical night' is foreign to the spirituality of the Orthodox Church". One would hesitate to disagree with such an eminent authority, but, while there is a real and legitimate diversity in this matter between the mystical charisms of

John in fact affirms that the soul undergoing this dark night is very profoundly imbued with these three theological virtues, that, indeed, it can see itself to have a great love for God and that it would give a thousand lives for him (c.f. *D.N.* II, 7, 7). If hell is understood as confirmed lovelessness, then the real state of this person—one might say "ontologically" (*habitualmente*)—is diametrically opposite to it. However, in terms of conscious experience, it is as though all the vast potential for bliss of this deified existence is locked up, concentrated within the "substance" of the soul and as yet unable to flow through the stream-beds of consciousness. To use John's own metaphor (II, 10, 6), for as long as the worker (God) has the iron of the soul in the furnace of his purifying love, its transformation into pure flamed-filled iron cannot be seen; only when he withdraws it occasionally from that furnace, "when contemplation assails it less vehemently", does the incandescence shine out in the soul's experience of enkindled love. John adds, of course, that until the purification is complete, such a period of consoling love can only be a temporary respite.

The second important note concerning this passive night of spirit is in regard to its being properly "spiritual" (in the scriptural sense of "concerning the Holy Spirit") or "theological" (in the literal sense of "God-meaning"). It is quite distinct from simply natural psychological trauma, even from that which is undergone in some genuine spirit of Christian faith and longsuffering. St.. John certainly allows that the enormous stress of this hidden purification may have strong and disconcerting reverberations in emotional turmoil, terrible feelings of uncertainty and loss of nerve—it's hardly to be expected that the experience of radical dispossession, of being driven by the Spirit beyond the limits of one's own resources, could allow a person to retain constant equanimity. Dismay leaves its mark in face and gesture. Where words fail, tears may flow as some relief (II, 9, 7). But behind the psychological symptoms lies a theological cause which is, quite simply,

East and West, it would seem to be a much less absolute difference than Lossky suggests. Other Orthodox theologians have perceived real lines of convergence between the "Dark Night" of John of the Cross and the "kenosis" or self-empting spirituality of a long line of Orthodox saints. c.f.—(Ask Author).

consuming love for God. That love, as we shall see more closely later, is itself a gift from God now overflowing the soul's capacity to contain or "cope with" it. And so, if in the earlier phase of the passive night of sense it was so important to discern the authenticity of contemplative darkness by distinguishing it from mere psychic lethargy or neurosis ("a kind of humour in the brain or heart" *D.N.* I, 13, 6), *a fortiori* here, where the stakes are so much higher. This passive night of spirit is a mode of existence which is wholly dependent upon a consuming relationship with God (though in the form of a desolating sense of absence); the psychological and emotional effects are simply that—effects or consequences of a real ontological relationship between God and the human person. Depth psychology may explore those effects; only theology, working by faith, can reach into that essential and transcendent relationship. If, then, the phenomena of the dark night are *per se* secondary, we should also observe that it gives a false colour to the issue to consider mere intensity of suffering as the essential mark of the passive night of spirit. While the suffering is indeed awesome, and St. John gives an account of it with a passionate intensity befitting the tragic-glorious world of sixteenth-century Spain, in no way does he endow the mere fact of suffering with a perverse mystique of its own. It has no meaning for him apart from its being a communion in the redemptive suffering of Christ:

> Let Christ crucified be enough for you, and with him suffer and rest; and for this reason be annihilated as to all things outward and inward.
>
> (*Points of Love*, 13)

A most apposite comment on this matter is from one who, by a sad irony, precipitated the whole nation of Spain into the terrible dark experience depicted in Goya's nightmarish war series: for Napoleon, "it is the cause not the suffering, which makes the martyr." It is love for God in the crucified Christ, not the pain of a crucifixion, which makes the dark night.

We observed earlier that this passive night of spirit is not a dimension of any Christian's experience of faith, but that it is a temporal stage in the unfolding of a life of holiness. It can only follow upon the active night of spirit/passive night of sense. Nevertheless, that chronological sequence is not demarcated with absolute clarity. For example, before the time of abundance of the active night of spirit is complete, the approach of the passive purification of spirit is announced by certain brief touches of radical deprivation, "tokens and heralds" of the full darkness to come, but which interrupt serene contemplative love only for brief periods (*D.N.* II, 1, 1). For one who does not respond with the total submission and abandonment necessary for complete purification, there will be a kind of stalemate at this transition point. A life of considerable contemplative grace will be punctuated by brief "morsels" of purifying darkness; but, unwilling to let go the beautiful activity of spirit which God has placed in his hands, such a one balks at entering the crucible of the principal passive night in which alone God's work of purification can be perfected. Again, we have already mentioned the brief periods of relief in the midst of the dark night proper, when God draws the iron of the soul out of the furnace of passive desolation to allow some ardent loving response to shine out "actively." These periods of spiritual liberty, however, are not unconditionally welcome. Positively, they are a foretaste of the perfect spiritual act for which the dark night is preparing the soul. On the other hand, the activity which marks these periods of relief is still slightly vitiated, and the soul, now with some awareness of the wonderful effects of the dark paralysing fire, is impatient for God to resume and complete his refining work (*D.N.* II, 10, 6; II, 10, 9).

Finally, while there is a genuine sequence in the different phases of the night, we should also recognize their integral connection and continuity. The purification of the senses begun in the earlier phases only comes to its perfection in the radical refinement of the spirit. If we envisage the grace of God moving progressively inwards, then the divinization of the outward sensitive life is not accomplished until the light has reached the innermost substance of the soul and from there irradiates the whole person. The earlier dialectic between passive night of sense and active spiritual discipline "serves rather to accomodate sense to spirit than to unite spirit to God" (*D.N.* II, 2, 1). It has to do more with the preliminary integration of the human powers among themselves, so that "it should be called a kind of correction and restraint of the desire rather than purgation" (*D.N.* II, 3, 1). Only when this initial reordering is to some extent achieved can the person in the wholeness of his human nature, sense and spirit, be directly subject to the purifying and illuminating action of God's "ray of darkness".

> The reason is that all the imperfections and disorders of the sensuous part have their strength and root in the spirit where all habits, both good and bad, are brought into subjection.
>
> (*Ibid*)

Thus it is true that the passive night of spirit follows upon that of sense, but in the manner of subsuming it into a higher mode and bringing it to its proper term.

The Summit of the Mount

The passage of the soul through these shades of night is a way towards the divine light of perfect union in love of God. St. John envisages it both as a way of inwardness to the depths of the soul and as an ascent upwards of the mount of perfection, towards the summit of the hierarchy of spiritual being. It is in the *Spiritual Canticle* (stanzas 13-40) and the *Living Flame* that he expounds those sublime reaches of "spiritual betrothal" and "spiritual marriage", so that these works can in some way be taken as a sequel to the *Ascent* and *Dark Night*.[8] As we have seen, one of the principal factors which distinguishes each of the nights is the variable interplay of activity

---

[8]This should not be taken as the necessary or even best programme of reading the works of St John. A wise Carmelite tradition, exemplified by St Therese of Lisieux in her instruction of novices, would turn first to the *Spiritual Canticle,* in which the whole perspective of spiritual growth is delineated and, even more important, the essential motive power of loving is more manifest. With the goal and climate of love thus firmly established, the way of the dark nights will be more truly understood as a way of *living* faith, that is, vitalized by the love of God. Without that, they are terribly misunderstood as a mere dogged spiritual endurance.

and passivity, of self-realization and dispossession of self. These have emerged as being far more complementary than they are opposed, and so now we should observe briefly how, in this final condition of being transformed in God through love, these two dimensions, of action and passivity, of attainment and dispossession, come together in a unique concord.

Just because the goal of transforming union follows upon a phase of radical passivity (passive night of spirit), it must not therefore be construed in a simplistic dialectic as being "active" with the kind of raw autonomy of earlier human initiative— that misconception of spiritual maturity as a 'coming of age' which asserts its independence. Neither is it the crown of absolute passivity—the contrary 'mystical' error of the Quietist or Illuminist, for whom the soul as perfect instrument of God must have nothing substantial left of its own proper activity. Certainly, there may now be more of those phenomena, not unknown in earlier phases, which depend wholly on the divine initiative and which must be left absolutely in the hands of him who infuses them, blessings which are impeded or spoiled "by no more than the slightest act which the soul may desire to make on its own account" (*L.F.* 3:41). However, these are extraordinary transient graces which do not habitually exclude the normal round of a person's natural activity. Moreover, even these graces in themselves do not imply a total inertia, because the activity which St. John forbids is that presumptuous initiative which would impose its own conditions on the work of God, a "desire" to work "on its own account" (*Ibid*). True Christian being and action, however, are not precluded by God's work. On the contrary, they have their very perfection through being wholly docile to him. And so, full mystical union brings to perfection both the work of God in the soul and the soul's own free cooperation.

> And the movements of this divine flame of love burning in the soul ... are not made only by the soul that is transformed in the flames of the Holy Spirit, neither are they made by him alone; but by the Spirit and the soul together, the Spirit moving the soul even as the fire moves the air that is enkindled.
>
> (*L.F.* 3:10)

We must explore that mystery of divinization more closely in the following chapter. Here we simply observe that this image of air transfigured by fire—the soul by the Holy Spirit—is an eloquent sign of who St John of the Cross is in himself and for us. It is true of each of the saints. The fulfillment of human life and freedom lies in being caught up, strengthened and transformed in the life and freedom of God. No one is more uniquely himself than when thus "lost" into God's power and glory.

Having outlined the general pattern of St John's exposition, we ought to recall an observation made earlier, and situate all this somewhat scholastic schematization into its true context of human growth, with all its ambivalence and obscurities. Precisely because authentic spirituality touches more closely upon the uniqueness of the individual person, its explanation cannot be reduced adequately to any general laws. And from the other, divine, point of view, the harmonious design of God's Wisdom at play in the children of men has a gratuitousness and freedom which transcend all abstract norms. For these reasons, to enter into the way of God's artistry in the contemplative life is to enter a realm which is quite beyond prediction:

> wherefore, upon this way, to enter upon the way is to leave the way. . . .
>
> (*Asc.* II, 4, 5)

The whole purpose of St John's 'system' is to release one's hold on all self-proposed systems and to be abandoned to the tracklessness of God's saving journey in the wilderness. Thus, although we rightly view his outline of the ascent to union as a sketch of his own spiritual likeness, it must be with the understanding that the original face itself was intensely alive and moving. Behind the apparent immobility of an icon there is the ceaseless play of Holy Wisdom in the saint. St John's writings are an icon of his own visage. Their formal structure must mediate, not conceal, the life of the Spirit that was in him.

4

Empty for God

Spiritual nakedness and poverty of spirit and emptiness in
faith is what is needed for union of the soul with God.

(*Asc.* II, 24, 9)

John of the Cross was driven in his life and his prayer by an
inexhaustible surge of vitality welling up from a source which
lay deeper than his own heart—

Its origin I know not—it has none,
But all origin, I know, is from here begun,
Although it is the night.

And yet an essential quality of that experience, hard to learn
yet inescapable, is that true growth in prayer is often effected
in weakness, inability and the exhaustion of one's own resources. This certainly does not mean a cultivated spiritual las-
situde. John's summons to the way of prayer and ascetic
discipline has an evangelical urgency that leaves no doubt
about the constant need of free self-giving. He dedicates himself
with all the generosity he can muster to the reordering and
purifying of his vital powers and to seeking out a new and
appreciative understanding of the ways of God in Christ.
Nevertheless, in a strangely disguised blessing which reflects
the scandal and folly of the Cross, such efforts of generosity
cannot but fail in their initial purpose.

> For, however much the beginner practises in himself the mortification of all his actions and passions, he can never achieve it completely, nor even very much at all, until God should work it in him passively by means of the purgation of this dark night.

(*D.N.* I, 7, 5)

All that one brings to bear of one's own powers must be radically insufficient.

But St. John would have no misunderstanding about the spirit of this 'failure'. "However much" one strives . . .: this is by no means a discouragement of ascetic zeal. On the contrary, behind this phrase lies John's assumption that the beginner should set out with all energy and hopefulness. Only thus can the blessed poverty of spirit be realized. For the greater his zeal, the more deeply will he experience the inadequacy of that zeal to reach its own perfection directly; and the more profoundly he experiences the poverty of his own resources, the more is he truly prepared to received the help of God "passively", which alone can bring him to his true goal. Eventually this latter moment of spiritual growth—the knowledge of God's powerful and merciful love—must entirely suffuse the experience of self. Only thus can the experience of the sheer inadequacy of human resources to reach perfection issue as it should, not in the open bitterness of despair or the disguised hardness of compromise and double standards, but in the perception of that divine care which heals all.

> But it is needful that the soul should seek to do as much as it can on its own part to become perfect, so that it might merit that God place it in that divine care in which it is healed of all that it was unable itself to cure.
>
> (*D.N.* I, 3, 3)

The tenderness which his brethren and penitents experienced from him, especially the sick, the neglected and those most aware of their poverty and frailty, was a reflection and mediation of what he knew himself to have received from

God. There is no trace of sentimentality here. God's coming to help the soul is a response to virile, though inadequate, action; the soul thus healed is not passive in the manner of pusillanimous dejection. Granted this, one can then safely add that the way of spiritual growth will certainly involve a spirit of docility. One must know one's need and be consciously disposed to receive correction:

> the imperfections into which they see themselves fall they suffer with humility and with meekness of spirit and loving fear of God, hoping in him.
>
> (*D.N.* I, 2, 8)

In suggesting that the soul might "merit" (*merezca*) God's saving help by generous striving, John is echoing one of the principal chords of sixteenth-century doctrinal debate and a major theme of Tridentine theology. A true estimation of his teaching must take into account this foundation of objective theological reality. For St. John, the spiritual life is not merely a matter of cultivating appropriate psychological attitudes, but of realizing in oneself the truth of personal being as revealed in Christ. The notion that he is a "spiritual" writer must not be taken in a too superficially psychological sense, as if distinguishing him absolutely from the "speculative" theologians who are supposedly concerned "merely" with metaphysical realities. This Castilian friar, formed in the theology faculty of Salamanca in the 1560s, cannot but have been deeply influenced by the Council of Trent's Decree on Justification (promulgated in 1547), with its insistence on the reality of the change brought about in man by God's merciful forgiveness. Martin Luther had interpreted—or at least was understood to have interpreted—the Pauline doctrine of justification by faith as a change in God's attitude towards man, effected by the obedience of Christ in his paschal mystery. In that classical Protestant doctrine, the intrinsic nature of man as sinner was thought not to be changed. "His faith is reckoned as righteousness" (Rom 4:5), and "reckoned" (*reputatur*) was understood in its literal and extrinsic sense, as though Abraham and his descendants in faith were merely considered by God to be holy, and were not in fact made so. Against this, Trent affirmed

that the unmerited and utterly free gift of God's justifying
grace constitutes a new mode of being, "a new creation", in the
human person (2 Cor 5:17). Moreover, in virtue of this real
change in man, won for him through his share in the paschal
mystery of Christ, he is truly able and obliged to cooperate
with the work of God for his own salvation—to "merit an
increase of grace" through his own good works performed "in
Christ".

　　Although he is not writing with polemical purpose, St. John
of the Cross clearly reflects these fundamental Tridentine
concerns, but he incorporates them into his teaching in a
particularly subtle way. As if in the crucible of his own life in
the Spirit, there emerges the real gold of Christian sanctity to
which the theology of grace bears witness. Firstly, his notion
of merit is not aggressive or presumptuous. There is a constant
concern for growth in the spiritual life, but it is a growth
measured as much by the soul's humbling as by the exaltation
of mystical gifts.

> We may also call this secret contemplation a ladder because,
> just as a ladder has steps in order to ascend, it has the same
> ones also for going lower; just so is it with this secret
> contemplation, for the same communications which it works
> in the soul to raise it up into God, also humble it in itself.
>
> 　　　　　　　　　　　　　　　　　　　　(*D.N.* II, 18, 2)

Thus, while he affirms that zeal merits an increase in God's
favour, it is equally true that it is not simply the reward of a
person's *success* in religious efforts. On the contrary, it is won
through efforts which in fact fail to achieve their full intended
perfection and, most importantly, which are *perceived* by the
person concerned to be so poor (". . . humble it in itself"). One
is indeed raised into God's presence, but there is no place there
for human "boasting" (c.f. Rom 3:27; Eph 2:8ff). The desire to
love and serve God should always exceed one's present cap-
ability, but by that very desire the devout person "merits" that
God should in his mercy stoop to rescue him in his weakness:
"the soul is healed of all that it was of itself unable to cure"
(*D.N.* I, 3, 3).

　　There is a further exceptional quality here in St. John's

doctrine. In an age when so much poor average Scholastic theology was prone to ossify in conceptualist categories, "which seemed to divorce the gift of grace from the Giver",[1] he always retains the essential meaning of grace as a living relationship between God and the human person. We have already re-marked that his spirituality is not merely a reduction to psychological categories. His knowledge of the effect of grace is of a reality which includes, but also far transcends, the conscious and unconscious realms which are susceptible of observation and analysis, "transforming and enlightening [the soul] as regards all its being and power and strength" (*L.F.* 1:13). Yet neither is his notion of grace a reduction to merely philosophical, ontic categories. The grace which the soul merits is a "being taken by God into that divine care" (*D.N.* I, 3, 3), a divinely personal cherishing which exceeds all calculation.

In this way, then, he traces growth towards religious per-fection not just in an ascending order of virtues and spiritual proficiency acquired through active ascesis and meditation, but also negatively, by a kind of anticipation—experienced as a present want or poverty—of that perfection towards which his efforts are directed but cannot of themselves attain. Indeed, the suffering of temptation and of one's own spiritual weakness can be an index of the fullness of grace for which God is preparing the soul.

> In proportion to the degree of love of union to which God desires to raise the soul, he will humble it more or less intensely, or in greater or less time.
>
> (*D.N.* I, 14, 5)

Just how concrete and practical is this humbling self-know-ledge, can be gathered from chapters two to eight of the first Book of the *Dark Night*. Here we have a masterpiece of unpretentious, realistic spiritual discernment in which, under the headings of the seven deadly sins, St. John exposes some of the imperfections of the zealous beginner. 'Progress' means to be brought to the painful recognition of one's hidden

---

[1] C. Ernst, *The Theology of Grace*, Dublin and Cork, 1974, p 61.

motives of absurd self-esteem and puerile acquisitiveness in the things of the spirit. Far from feeling complacently proficient, the soul is brought through contemplative aridity into an habitual sense of its need for purification,

> considering itself now as nothing and having no satisfaction in itself; for it sees that of itself it does nothing, nor can do anything.
>
> (*D.N.* I, 12, 2)

And so the need for passive purification is most immediately apparent in each person's experience of his own moral condition. Habits of sin impair those very powers of mind and heart which are our only resources of spirituality: a darkened mind cannot know how to dispel its own blindness, an enfeebled will cannot will itself to love perfectly. At its very best the soul needs to be saved, is dependent upon another Spirit of holiness, the gift of God's grace, to be rescued from its futility. In St. John's Dark Night this logical and doctrinal principle becomes a vivid fact of conscious experience. Moreover, the purity which is demanded for mystical union with God is not just ethical: or we might rather say that the full reality of moral purity will include not only a person's behaviour, but will also have deeper resonances in the quality of his being which is the source of that behaviour. St. John is writing neither as a psychologist nor as a metaphysician. His is a more global approach, an exploration into the reaches of man's spirit which is at the same time speculative and experiential. His 'doctrine' is in fact a statement of that existential reality where consciousness and being meet. The meaning of selflessness in John's writing will be determined by this coalescence of the psychological, moral and metaphysical, and nowhere does it appear more clearly than in his cardinal notion of "emptiness" (*vacio*).

The essential preparation for union with God is that the soul "must be emptied (*se ha de vaciar*) of all that can fall within its capacity" (*Asc.* II, 4, 2). Spanish and Latin are similar enough to see here a direct echo of the great monastic ideal of *vacare Deo*, being free for God, but St. John takes it up in a rather specialized way. Although this notion had always been used in close association with mysticism and contemplative prayer, it most commonly designated a 'state of life', *vita contemplativa,* of which the actual experience of contemplative prayer was only one component, even though perhaps the crowning one. It indicated that spaciousness of regulated monastic life which helps to free the monk from the clutter of particular anxieties and to inform his life with the tranquility of a quiet round of prayer, *lectio* and work. Typical of this mediaeval sense of *vacare Deo* is the way St. Bernard contradistinguishes it from external busy activity: "By no means should one who is at leisure to attend to God (*qui vacat Deo*) aspire to the tumultous life of the officials of the monastery".[2] It envisages a certain hiddenness and external uneventfulness, a 'holy leisure' (*divinum otium*); it moulds the temporality of human existence into an image of eternity (*vita angelica*); it is the whole of a person's life given over freely and consciously in religious consecration, "empty *for God*".

St. John of the Cross knew and valued that wholeness of consecration in his own Carmelite religious life, whether in the solitude of El Calvario in the Sierra Morena or in the urban monasteries of Alcalá and Beas. Nevertheless, the focus of his attention is concentrated upon the inward harmony and simplicity which the external ascesis is meant to achieve, and this, not so much in the habitual tranquility which is to pervade all the monastic exercises, but in the stillness and emptiness of contemplative prayer.

> And let him not meddle in forms, meditations and imaginings, or anything discursive, lest his soul be disquieted and shaken out of its contentment and peace.... He is doing no small thing in pacifying the soul and bringing it into rest and peace, without any work or desire, which is what Our Lord asks us through David, saying: *Vacate, et videte quoniam ego sum Deus* (Ps 45:11, Vulgate). As if he had said: 'Learn to be empty of all things, that is to say, inwardly and outwardly, and you will see that I am God'.
>
> (*Asc.* II, 15, 5)

---

[2]*Serm. de assumpt. B.V.M.,* iii, 2. Quoted in Cuthbert Butler, *Western Mysticism,* London: Constable, 1967, pp 191f.

Another feature of St. John's doctrine of 'emptiness', one which deserves special notice in our age so hopeful of finding efficient spiritual techniques, is that it is fundamentally sheer grace of God rather than a matter of a person's own spiritual contriving. The process of emptiness itself falls under that constant spiritual law by which human resources ultimately stand in need of redemption. It involves a dialectic of active ascesis and passive sanctification. Thus, the first moment or phase is of deliberate, free, unconditional striving: "The soul must empty itself (*ha de vaciarse*) perfectly and willingly . . . so far as it is able" (*Asc.* II, 4, 2). The second, passive, moment envelopes and completes the first: "But the soul must be emptied (*se ha de vaciar*) of every kind of thing which can fall within its capacity" (*Ibid*). The "perfectly" of the active ascesis clearly pertains to an unqualified zealous intention, and not to its actual accomplishment, for besides the attaining of union with God, there is nothing "so difficult that it lies beyond human powers and strength, namely, to throw off with natural power that which is natural" (*Asc.* III, 2, 13). Although an orientation towards transcendence is an intrinsic feature of our spiritual being, we are quite unable to realize out of our own resources that transcendent life to which we are called, or even to dispose ourselves adequately. We may well be capable of a merely negative suppression or suspension of the natural order of image and concept, but to this self-induced emptiness St. John ascribes no religious value. Whatever natural value it might have as psychic repose, without God's gift of his Spirit in contemplative faith, "it would do nothing and have nothing" (*Asc.* II, 14, 6). A cultivated emptiness in prayer is not the sublime "nothing" of the experience of the transcendent Form which embraces and dissolves all particular forms (c.f. *Asc.* II, 3, 1), but a vacuous counterfeit of authentic *vacare Deo*.

If the human task of disposing oneself in emptiness must be a matter of free assent, no less free must be the work of God by which he inspires and makes effective man's ascesis. Great care is needed in interpreting St. John in this matter because of his striking insistence that divine illumination must "necessarily" follow upon such emptiness.

And, being emptied in this way of all things so that it is

empty and dispossessed of them (which, as we have said, is what the soul is able to do), it is impossible, if it does what it can, that God should fail to do his own part by communicating himself to the soul, at least secretly and in silence. It is more impossible that the sun should fail to shine in a serene and unclouded sky

(*L.F.* 3:46)

This image of divine light shining through clear air or a perfectly clear window is a favourite one of St. John's,[3] and in every case it illustrates the inevitable connection between emptiness of spirit and divine infusion.

But does this not seem to be an infringement of God's sovereign freedom, as though his graces could be compelled by some creaturely condition? Moreover, in spite of what we have seen about genuine emptiness being a gift of grace, it seems here to be a preparation worked primarily by man which calls down divine blessings "... it is what the soul is able to do". Equally problematic seems to be the kind of passivity by which the soul receives this grace. Its only activity seems to be in removing the obstacles to the light, which will then flood the soul 'automatically', without any truly human dimension in the act of acceptance. Such passivity would take no account of a person's freedom at the heart of accepting or refusing God's gift. It is more akin to the determinism of physical phenomena:

> when the soul has attained to purifying and emptying itself of all forms and imaginings that can be grasped, it will remain in this pure and simple light, ... For the enamoured soul, lacking what is natural, is then infused with the divine, so that there may be no vacuum in nature.
>
> (*Asc.* II, 15, 4)

This passage exmplifies the perennial problem of metaphor in spiritual discourse, wherein it can be overlooked that what is at issue is in fact a supremely personal relationship between

---

[3]c.f. *Asc.* II, 5, 7; II, 14, 9; II, 16, 10; *D.N.* II, 8, 3; *Cant.* 26:17.

man and God. And 'personal' must be taken here in its highest
sense of achieved living communion. It is not as though man
might us his 'personal' powers for self-perfection in order to
manipulate blessings from God. It is not a bargain being struck
between two intelligent but detached parties, one winning a
moral advantage over the other. It is a relationship of love,
which is constantly and radically formed by the motive of
giving rather than taking.

> To seek oneself in God is clean contrary to love. For to seek
> oneself in God is to seek delights and refreshments from
> God; but to seek God in oneself is not only to desire to be
> without both of these for God's sake, but to be inclined to
> choose for Christ's sake all that is most distasteful, in regard
> to God and to the world, and this is love of God
>
> (*Asc.* II, 7, 5)

This reiterated 'for God's sake, ... for Christ's sake' is no
mere pious formula. It is a measured and literal statement of
the fundamental intention that must shape all Christian existence, which finds its centre and source of meaning no longer
in itself but in "him that I most love" (*Cant. 2*). Such love, for
all its passionate urgency, imposes no conditions. It has a
clarity and delicacy which belong only to a total trusting of
oneself into the will of the Beloved. Thus, as the Blessed Virgin
at Cana ("They have no wine" Jn 2:3) and the sisters of Lazarus
("Lord, he whom you love is sick" Jn 11:3), just so, such love
expresses its prayerful dependence simply as a trustful and
unqualified unveiling of self in need before him:

> The soul does no more than present her need and affliction
> to the Beloved. For he who loves with sensitivity (*discreta-
> mente*) has no concern to beg for what he lacks and desires,
> but only reveals his need so that the Beloved may do what
> seems right to him.
>
> (*Cant.* 2:8)

Thus, the movement into spiritual emptiness is, amazingly,
most truly a growth and a flourishing and not a spiral of
disintegration. In the Gospel's unique wisdom—foolishness to

the world—one loses one's life only to find it in Christ the Beloved; it declares no other way for a human person to become whole than that he should freely commit himself into God's pre-eminent, loving, transforming will. It makes no sense apart from love. Nor does it make sense—and this distinguishes it from all this—worldly love—without that gift of God which provides man with the very means by which he can thus 'realize himself' divinely.

> The soul lives where it loves rather than in the body which it animates, because it does not have its life in the body—rather, it gives life to the body—and lives through love in God whom it loves.
>
> (*Cant.* 8:3)

In the way of spiritual emptiness the soul asserts nothing of its own. It recognizes the will of the Beloved as the unique source of all meaning, and so, freely relinquishing control of its life to Him, enters into a region not of uncertainty, but indeed of great mystery. This is true of every genuine personal relationship of love, but it is eminently so in relationship with the transcendent God of absolute freedom. However sublime and authentic the communion with God might be, "in truth, he is still hidden from the soul, and therefore it is always fitting that, with regard to all these sublime things, the soul should consider him to be hidden and should seek him as hidden, saying: 'Where have you hidden yourself'" (*Cant.* 1:3). Nevertheless, it is extremely important for a true understanding of St. John's notion of mystery that it should be seen as *transcending* man's reason, that is, as surpassing his comprehension, but not flatly denying it. The emptiness of spirit which he proclaims, the total docility to God's action, is not a blind acquiescence to futility in the face of an inscrutable and tyrannical Divine Will. We may speak of the awesome and consuming nature of the *via negativa,* but not of its absurdity. And so, the contemplative way, "to proceed by not understanding rather than by desiring to understand" (*Asc.* II, 8, 5), must itself be intelligible—firstly, in a transcendent sense, as proceeding from the fullness of divine Wisdom for man, and also in an accessible form, as standing in harmony with his own nature. In these two ways the unsearchable mystery of God's saving design is manifested, not dispelling the darkness but filling it with powerful meaning and direction.

The revelation of this spiritual way is not in abstract principles, but in a concrete person, Wisdom itself incarnate in Jesus Christ and spelt out in his Paschal mystery. He is the theologically unifying principle of St. John's mystical experience and doctrine. We will explore this more closely when we come to the actual form of union with God. But a true spiritual portrait of St. John of the Cross must also include a certain consonance between the Gospel doctrine of salvation through loving self-dispossession and what we can know of our own human nature. Through this harmony or analogy, the dark night of dispossession has its own intrinsic beauty and peace, "more lovely than the dawn" (*D.N.* 4). Without it, the sheer commitment of faith, unsupported as it is meant to be by any natural calculation, would take on a jagged edge of blind desperation. Its likely fruits would be resentment, anger and despair. Such a figure is utterly unlike "the soul" of St. John of the Cross. Although he speaks of long periods of the most desolating sense of abandonment, when it seems that his natural existence is being completely undone—(and we can presume that he was not spared all distressing manifestations of such inner trials—groans, agitation and the partial relief of tears) (*D.N.* II, 6, 1; 9, 7)—still, even these moments have their meaningful place within a total pattern of divine-humane flourishing. John emerged from the trial of emptiness marked by courage, sensitive compassion and a more profound, unassailable peace which was quite palpable to those near him.

And so, even as he turns to the transcendent, unconditional quality of contemplative faith, John does not make it a sheer blind assertion. Rather, "it is fitting that we should demonstrate (*probemos*)" how no created reality, and therefore no natural power of man, can be a direct means of union with God (*Asc.* II, 8, 1). While the mystery can in no way be exhaustively explained, there can be a very real perception and demonstration by cogent reasons (*razones*) of how appropriate (*conveniente*) is the way of dark faith to man's growth in divine union. Even where human intelligence is to be entirely transcended, it is always respected. The argument can be reduced to the following simple form. All created reality is, in a fundamental way, quite unlike God who is its transcendent Source. But to attain to a certain goal, the means must have a true connection with and resemblance to that goal. It follows that every human experience, even the most sublime mystical intimation, insofar as it is comprehended within that person's own existence, must fall short of God himself:

> No supernatural knowledge or apprehension in this mortal state can serve as a proximate means to the high union of love with God. For all that can be understood by the intellect, and tasted by the will, and contrived by the imagination, is very unlike God and disproportionate to him.
>
> (*Asc.* II, 8, 5)

To reinforce this general principle, St. John devotes many chapters of the *Ascent of Mount Carmel* (Book II, 15-32) to the exposition of such mystical graces. The very competence and sublimity of his account, clearly based on his own personal experience, gives authority to his ultimate judgement that "all must be rejected (*se niegen*)".[4]

This "denial" is not a spiritual nihilism. In fact, paradoxical though it may seem, it sustains a certain orientation in the darkness, a profounder sense of meaning for the spiritual emptiness. It can do this because, while directing the soul continuously beyond itself into the trackless regions of faith, it still takes its beginning from where the soul is now. The denial which anticipates a new degree of perfection is at the same time an implicit affirmation of the reality, though insufficient, of the present attainment. A hope which is able to "risk" all is the sign of a profound security. St. John uses to advantage the traditional image of the ladder of spiritual ascent. Each indi-

---

[4]*Asc.* II, 26, 18. Only in regard to the supreme kind of mystical intuitions of God does St. John allow that the soul need not behave in the same negative manner as in all the rest. These perceptions "come only to the soul which attains to union with God, because they themselves are that very union; for to have them means that the soul has a certain touch of the Divinity" (*Asc.* II, 26, 5). Nevertheless, as we shall see, even this is not really an exception to his principle of total self-dispossession, because the experience itself is of pure transcendence.

vidual step, taken in isolation, is simply remote from the
summit. Its true meaning lies in its being a means to reach that
goal; "and if the climber did not leave the steps behind him
until none were left, and if he desired to remain on any one of
them, he would never arrive nor mount to the level and
peaceful room which is the goal" (*Asc.* II, 12, 5). Just so, the
cardinal error which frustrates growth in the spiritual life is to
rest content with any degree of attained perfection. No matter
how sublime, every step in the spiritual ascent must be experienced as the point of a new departure into a further realm of
new grace. The authenticity of every particular experience of
God is found precisely in its intrinsic, insistent summons to
self-transcendence.

John's demand for a constant movement of selflessness is of
exceptional importance in the light of the prevailing spirit of
his age—and still more so for our own. With St. Teresa of
Avila and St. Ignatius of Loyola, he is one of the great
Conquistadores of the inner, subjective realms of religious
experience. Their extraordinary reflective perception and refined analysis of individual psychological phenomena stand in
contrast with the greater universality of an earlier mystical
tradition—the "Western Mysticism" which Dom Cuthbert
Butler traces through St. Augustine, St. Gregory the Great
and St. Bernard.[5] Now, while St. John shares this feature of
psychological introspection to an eminent degree, it is always
(as it is in the other great saints) in the service of a way of
prayer which points constantly beyond the self towards God.
His analysis of concrete experience is of its nature of the
subject—in this sense "subjective" or "existential"—but he
never tires of insisting that the meaning of that experience is
not immanent in the subject but derives wholly from its
reference to the Other, to God. Indeed, he reserves some of his
most trenchant criticism for those who make their own spiritual "state" the object of prime concern:

> As these beginners feel themselves to be so fervent and
> diligent in spiritual things and devout exercises ... they

[5] *Op. cit.*

qol 52300

come to have some satisfaction with their works and with themselves.... Sometimes they feel like letting others know how spiritual and devout they are, and for this purpose they occasionally give outward signs in movements, sighs and other ceremonies.... Some of them also make little of their faults, and at other times become over-sad when they see themselves fall into them, thinking themselves to be saints already.

(*D.N.* I, 2, 1-5)

Here is the relentless spiritual master. We might easily be moved to scorn by his incisive irony, which would be all the more devastating given the *honra,* the inflated self-worth, which St. Teresa laments was so prevalent in their world. And yet we must recall that such imperfections arise from the discovery of quite genuine spiritual gifts. His irony is tempered by the understanding that God's spiritual gifts sometimes so exceed our present ability to receive them rightly that they inevitably bring in their train impurities of motive (*D.N.* I, 1, 3; I, 7, 5). The spiritual poverty which the Gospel calls for is not detachment from external things but from one's own personal existence; therefore, St. John insists, an experience of authentic spiritual illumination can become a fetter and a burden if the soul does not immediately look beyond it in an aspiration of self-transcendence, "freeing and disencumbering itself completely in that which pertains to the spirit" (*Asc.* II, 7, 3). Even the realities of our own life which God himself has formed in us through grace are subject to the law of renunciation; "God alone is the one who must be sought and won" (*Ibid*).

The contemplative wisdom of John of the Cross thus displays two most distinctive features. He maintains a resolute, dynamic intention always beyond his present appropriated spiritual condition into a region of more profound communion, dark but lovingly compelling: that spiritual instinct "guided me to where there awaited me One whom I well knew—a region where no one appeared".

(*D.N.* st 4) Where no one appeared (donde nadie parecía)!. That ever-deepening communion is always in this life, of faith—not a progressive manifestation of the Beloved hidden from everyone else, but an experienced Presence which itself is dark, non-appearing ("apophatic"). The second feature follows from the first. Because that actual dynamism of prayer is itself a transcending of the natural limits of human understanding and will, its origin must lie deeper than his own resources. Contemplation is essentially an action received.

> And thus it is that contemplation, by which the intellect has the highest perception of God, is called mystical theology, which means secret wisdom of God; because it is secret to the very intellect that receives it. For that reason St. Dionysius calls it 'a ray of darkness'.
>
> (*Asc.* II, 8,6; *De Myst. Theol,* c. 1, para 1)

For St. John, this dark, transcending power is given in the theological virtues, and pre-eminently in "faith".

5

Theological Virtues—
"By the Secret Ladder, Disguised"

St. John of the Cross locates the most fundamental presence of God in "the substance of the soul".[1] While that term belongs originally to a more philosophical Scholastic theology, John has written from within a mystical tradition which invests it with a meaning of concrete spiritual experience. It is in the deeper region of personal being which is the fountain-head of consciousness that the soul receives the "touch" of God:

> although these visions of spiritual substances cannot be unveiled nor clearly seen in this life by the understanding, they can nevertheless be felt in the substance of the soul, with the sweetest touches and unions, all of which pertain to spiritual feelings.
>
> (*Asc.* II, 24, 4)

The language of "touch" and "feeling" is significant. In the ground of personal being which underlies his reflective knowledge and deliberate action, he is simply and immediately receptive or passive to God's initiative.

On the other hand, arising out of that substance of the soul there are the "faculties", man's various capacities for personal action and initiative. Now, whilst God's gift of himself appears

---

[1] *Asc.* II, 5, 2; *D.N.* II, 6, 4; 13, 3; *Cant.* 1:6; 14:12-18; *L.F.* 1:17; 2:10; 2:34; 3:69.

to be very much in harmony with the naturally receptive quality of the substance of the soul, the theological virtues, which purify and sanctify the faculties of spiritual action, are most commonly represented by St. John not so much as a development but as a drastic reversal of their natural operations.

> These three virtues all cause emptiness in the faculties: faith in the intellect causes an emptiness and darkness with respect to understanding; hope in the memory causes emptiness of all possessions; and charity causes emptiness in the will and detachment from all affection and from rejoicing in all that is not God.
>
> (*Asc.* II, 6, 2)

By this emptiness the theological virtues are the means by which the soul is "united to God according to its faculties" (*Asc.* II, 6, 1). Because that union is so totally a gift, our cardinal role is to be utterly receptive to it; hence, paradoxically, the perfection of our powers of action is wrought in a kind of emptying of their natural energy. John uses characteristically strong language for it. In the way of contemplation the theological virtues demand an "annihilation of the faculties according to their operation" (*Asc.* II, 6, 1), "a denial of the natural jurisdiction and operation of the faculties so that they may become capable of infusion and illumination from supernatural sources" (*Asc.* II, 6, 2).

This strong negative dimension of the virtues appears to be very different from the common notion of them as new powers of action—of knowing God and his truth, of hoping for his glory, of loving him and one's neighbour in the strength of the Holy Spirit. John, however, clearly states that his own account is concerned with the particular form that grace takes experientially in the *via negativa* of contemplative prayer (*Asc.* II, 13-15; *D.N.* I, 1, 1). He does not deny these virtues to be powers of action; rather, he gives the notion a particularly profound meaning. In the *Ascent* and in *Dark Night* I, there is a constant stream of exhortation that "the soul must acquire these three virtues" (*Asc.* II, 6, 5). This is the spiritual night which he calls "active, for the soul does what it can for its part to enter into it" (*Asc.* II, 6, 5), but it is an action which is primarily a matter of holding oneself in "emptiness" and attentive receptivity to God's dark presence.

> The soul, then, will frequently find itself in this loving and peaceful attentive presence (*asistencia*) without working in any way with its faculties—that is, with regard to particular acts—not working actively but only receiving.
>
> (*Asc.* II, 15, 2)

This steady commitment of attentiveness into the dark region where God is spiritually "sensed" is what John means by "acquiring" contemplative faith. Moreover, he makes it clear that, unlike naturally acquired virtues, whose growth is simply dependent on and proportioned to the practice of them, the growing power of faith, hope and love is always a free gift. While there is a sense in which practice makes one more adept in turning at will to this simple loving gaze into the divine mystery and away from determinate forms, that gaze itself is the effect of God's sustaining grace.

> Withdrawing the will from all apparent signs and testimonies, [the soul] is exalted in purest faith, which God increases and infuses in it much more intensely; and together with this He increases within it the other two theological virtues, which are charity and hope.
>
> (*Asc.* III, 32, 4)

These spiritual powers are at once the core of John's spiritual living and yet cause him to reach beyond every present limit of his own experience. If so much beyond him both in origin and goal, they must be given. In the night of contemplation the soul is being awakened into relationship by the touch of God.

Faith

O crystalline fount,
If on this your silvered surface

> *You might suddenly form*
> *The desired eyes*
> *Which I hold outlined in my depths.*
>
> *(Cant.* 12)

It would scarcely be possible to speak of St. John at all without reference to 'faith', so much does it stand at the centre of his doctrine. It is the only means to union with God, the only adequate horizon for true knowledge of oneself and the world. And so we have already traced many of its features, especially as regards its role in John's theology of Creation and in some of the principle forms of activity and passivity in contemplative prayer. Consequently, this section will serve to complement what has already been said with a few further important questions.

Firstly, a question of perspective. We have already noted John's peculiar emphasis on the passive mode of experiencing the virtues, an emphasis deriving from his dominant concern with contemplation. And these virtues, especially faith, are so deeply tied in with contemplative prayer that they might appear even to become synonymous with it:

> We go on now to treatment of the second part of this night [by which second part he means the entrance into contemplation (c.f. above, pp 67f)] *which is faith.*
>
> (*Asc.* II, 2, 1)

Indeed, so constant is his virtual identification of the night of faith with the night of contemplation that the question must arise: is faith exclusively, or at least only properly, expressed in contemplative prayer? That implication would seem to gain force from the complete omission of any mention of the theological virtues in the 'active night of sense', in which the Christian begins his ascent to perfection. What is demanded of the 'beginner' is simply resolution and fortitude in ascetical self-denial, and perseverance in the way of discursive meditation—this latter being assigned to the low realm of 'sense' and apparently involving only the natural imagination and reason (*Asc.* II, 12, 3; *D.N.* I, 8, 3). John offers no positive assurance that such exercises, for all their 'natural' and 'active' quality, may be deeply animated by faith, hope and love. Only in the second night, when the soul is becoming proficient in contemplative prayer, does he invoke the theological virtues, and these then become the very substance of prayer and the spiritual life as the soul "leans upon" nothing but them, "leaving behind" its earlier images and concepts. At first sight, then, one might suspect an elitist notion that 'true' faith belongs only to the elect few admitted to contemplation.

But for a correct understanding of his doctrine we must not isolate his special emphases from the wider perspective in which, however summarily, he sets them. Thus, at the head of his exposition of the night of faith we find, not a brilliantly original insight drawn from personal mystical wisdom, but a prosaic and generalized Scholastic definition:

> Faith, say the theologians, is a habit of the soul, certain and obscure ... [which] makes us believe truths revealed by God himself, which transcend all natural light and exceed all human understanding, beyond all proportion.
>
> (*Asc.* II, 3, 1)

The very awkwardness of this Scholastic intrusion (' ...as the theologians say... ') reveals John's readiness to accept a rather uncongenial formulation as a basis of his own teaching. It indicates a willing dependence upon a traditional understanding larger than his own. Even though he immediately proceeds to make use of this doctrine for his own purpose, as a rationale for the experience of contemplation, by elaborating on the transcendent nature of faith and the natural understanding being 'overwhelmed' in thick darkness by this excessive light, yet the principle is still firmly fixed: the dark night of contemplation is but one dimension of that "believing truths revealed by God" which is common to all Christian faith, even the most elementary. That, of course, is because "believing truths... " is always dependent upon the more fundamental action or, better, way of being, of believing in God, of surrendering oneself to him.

And as faith grows, formulated credal statements are not discarded in favour of an entirely unthematic consent to mystery. In the *Canticle*, expounding the sublime desire for the high mystical grace of spiritual betrothal, he readily acknowledges that the contemplative's faith will include the mundane dimension of a formulated profession of belief:

> The propositions and articles which faith sets before us she calls a silvered surface.
>
> (*Cant.* 12:4)

In this life it must be so. Only when faith comes to an end in the beatific vision will its "golden substance" be seen, stripped of that silver veil of conceptual formulation. To presume to transcend the *symbolum* of faith in this life would be futile presumption. We should consider two important corollaries arising out of this notion of faith; namely, its communal or ecclesial content, manifested by the verbal transmission of "the silver surface", and the divine reality of its object, "the golden substance" of God himself.

Firstly, then, the Church as the *community* of faith. It would be a grave distortion to regard St. John's contemplative faith as some kind of purely interior gnosis which supersedes external revelation and dogma. As we noticed in the Introduction, in each of the Prologues to his major mystical treatises there is a very strong affirmation of the normative guidance of Scripture and the Church's teaching. He explicitly denies that his own contemplative knowledge could be a sure guide in the things of the spirit: the Dark Night of faith is itself to be interpreted only by the higher principles of revelation. To suggest that such a profession is merely a courteous tactic designed to mollify an over-zealous Inquisition, and not a genuine statement of faith in the Church's teaching, would be so to question his integrity as to render the whole of his writing quite untrustworthy. He was no sycophant willing to get into print at the cost of compromising his own convictions. Moreover, as we shall see, this obedience to a living tradition is in fact most consistent with the whole of his mystical doctrine.

An important element in this profession is that the guidance of external revelation is to be invoked *especially* "in what is most important and dark for the understanding" (*Asc.* Prol. 2). The more deeply contemplative the experience, the greater its need for magisterial guidance. More so than others, the genuine mystic will have a healthy fear of self-delusion and will want to test his experience against the belief of the Church. Such an insistence will appear to be an authoritarian and rationalist reversal of true values, if doctrine is thought of as merely external and institutional as against the interior, profound and immediate knowledge of the mystic. But for St. John, the Church's dogma is a formulation of all the riches hidden in Christ, and the mystic's wisdom is simply a personal discovery of those (*Cant.* 37:4). Georges Morel puts it well:

> Consequently, there is no abdication (in the pejorative sense) by mystical experience in the face of Scripture and the Church: to the extent that the individual goes forth from himself along the spiritual nights, so does he enter by very experience more and more into the substance of the Church, into its reality which is Reality manifesting itself under the form of time.[2]

Morel thus shows a fine appreciation of John's sharing in the wisdom of the Scriptures mediated by the Church. However, he seems to fall into a reduced notion of the Church and a mistake in evaluating John's intentions, when he argues that John submits the *formulation* of his experience to the Church, but not the experience itself. This runs counter to all that John has to say against trusting, not only in one's conceptual judgements, but, even more dangerously, in one's own experience or in that of any individual, which is independent of the lived communion of the Church:

> I do not pretend to affirm anything that is mine by trusting to my own experience (*fiandome de experiencia*) or to that of any other spiritual persons.
>
> (*Cant.* Prol. 4)

---

[2] *Le sens de l'existence selon Saint Jean de la Croix*, Vol 1, Paris, 1960, p. 199.

The notion that "experience" is somehow self-explanatory and
infallible is probably the most common source of religious
illusion; and, one might add, the present age's fascination with
subjective phenomena and the premium value given to sincerity
make it particularly prone to that danger. John of the Cross's
strictures against individualistic self-approbation are a timely
caution. Mistaken ideas are dangerous in the spiritual life, but
aberrant experience is even more personally destructive, and
incorrigible by the individualist:

> He that falls and is blind will not, in his blindness, rise up
> alone; and if he rises up alone he will journey to where it is
> not fitting.
>
> (*Sayings* 11)

Precisely because it is a matter of lived experience, contemplation must willingly take its place within the wider mysteries
of the Incarnation, the whole Mystical Body and the communion of saints:

> and so we must now be guided in all things by the law of
> the man Christ and of his Church and ministers
>
> (*Asc.* II, 22, 7)

We can hardly presume that John would have absolved himself
from an obedience which he saw enjoined on all members of
the Church, even on Peter himself, "prince of the Church"
(*D.N.* I, 10, 1). For that obedience is not an oppressive,
belittling subjection, but gives access to the shared wisdom of
the whole Body of Christ. Therefore, the faith "which guided
me more surely than the light of noonday" (st. 4) is more than
the apophatic way of the individual's interior experience. It
includes also the objective component of '*the* faith' to be
believed, that greater mystery of revelation which must illumine
and guide the contemplative no less than the catechumen.

   That element of *receiving* provides the bridge between the
outward dogmatic and the interior contemplative strands. Such
is St. John's reverence for revelation in Scripture and Tradition

that we might well speak of it as 'mystical' in a wider sense of the word, for he has a very lively sense of the sublime passivity inherent in man's being addressed by the word of God. A common terminology reveals the continuity of doctrine and prayer. Thus, just as the soul is "most surely *guided*" by the ray of darkness in contemplation, so John submits all that he writes (an objectification of all that he *does* in prayer) "to the better judgement and understanding of our holy Mother the Roman Catholic Church, with whose *guidance* no man goes astray" (*L.F.* Prol. 1). Again, just as the soul in contemplative prayer must rely on no "supports" (*arrimos*) of its own experience but only on dark faith, so, in expounding this prayer, John "relies upon" (*arrimandome*) only the sources of Christian revelation (*L.F.* Prol. 1). Moreover, this is all perfectly consistent, for the very nature of the dark night of contemplation, with its complete self-abnegation, demands that the soul should go forward "trusting neither in my own experience nor in that of other spiritual persons" (*Cant.* Prol. 4). The support and guide of all experience of faith, is the faith of the Church.

In this respect, then, the interior and personal dark night of the soul has a profound and necessary ecclesial context. True, St. John provides a strong contrast with the other great Carmelites, St. Teresa of Avila and St. Thérèse of Lisieux, in not manifesting the apostolic value of prayer as a most powerful force for growth in the Church. His emphasis is on the fact that in contemplation more than in any other realm of Christian living the believer stands exposed as a unique individual before God, unable to hide himself in the supposed anonymity of being merely one member of a great crowd. Relationship with God here grows and is consummated in terms of pure and immediate presence—*monos pros Monon*—alone before the Alone:

> In solitude she lived And in solitude now has built her nest, And in solitude her dear one alone guides her, Who likewise in solitude was wounded by love.

For the soul that desires God is in no wise comforted by

> any company whatsoever, but all things make and cause
> within it greater solitude until it finds Him.
>
> (*Cant.* 35, para. 3; 36:1)

Nevertheless, even for St. John it is still the Church who is the
original Bride of Christ and who is always the first contemplative hearer of the Word of God. Commenting on the verse
of the psalm, 'Day to day pours forth speech, and night to
night utters knowledge' (Ps 19:2), he observes that

> the night, which is faith in the Church Militant, where it is
> still night [as distinct from the 'day' of beatific vision of the
> Church Triumphant], shows knowledge to the Church, and
> consequently (*por consiguiente*) to every soul, which knowl-
> edge is night to it.
>
> (*Asc.* II, 3, 5)

The mystic is no individualist following his own sublime
interior way independently of the prosaic, dogmatically bound
community. The Church is the primary recipient of God's
revelation in His Word: only as a member of that Body,
'consequently', does the individual receive the luminous darkness of faith. And there is absolutely no circumstance which
could legitimately withdraw the contemplative from his dependence on the Church, not even a personal revelation which
apparently 'confirms' the common doctrine:

> Even though the truths already revealed to [the soul] be
> revealed again, it will believe them not because they are
> now revealed anew, but because they have already been
> sufficiently revealed to the Church: indeed, it must close its
> understanding to them, holding simply to the doctrine of
> the Church and to its faith, which as St. Paul says, enters
> through hearing.
>
> (*Asc.* II, 27, 4: Rom 10:17)

On two other occasions John alludes to this verse from

Romans,[3] and each time it is used to corroborate his argument that the fine point of faith, the consent given to God's truth, is elicited immediately by the preaching of Christ, either personally as with the first disciples, or through the ministry of his Church to later believers. In the complex fabric of actual believing there will of course be other dimensions of experience—various qualities of feeling, of the sense of knowing or of mystery—but these will be ancillary, not essentially constructive of faith. The contribution of natural understanding is to be "brought into subjection and blinded",

> For, as St. Paul says, *fides ex auditu,* as if to say: faith is not knowledge which enters by any of the senses, but only the consent of the soul to what enters through the ear.
>
> (*Asc.* II, 3, 3)

Such a sentence might lead one to suspect the adequacy of John's philosophical epistemology, but his doctrinal point is clear; faith is received only in a totally obedient hearing of God's word, and the ecclesial context is a necessary condition for the perfection of self less consent.

Granted, then, that St. John's notion of faith includes the believing of doctrine proclaimed by the Gospel and the tradition of the Church, and in that sense is specifically *Christian* faith, we must still face a further crucial question: *how* is that dimension of the Christian Creed related to the actual practice of 'dark', non-conceptual, 'contemplative faith'? Apart from the fact that it might well be the same person who both professes a formulated Christian belief and who reaches by a simple loving intention towards the unseen, incomprehensible God, is there any intrinsic connection between these two activities? Is there anything essentially Christian about St. John's dark night of faith?

The problem arises in a practical way from two different points of view. On the one hand, there are many non-Christian, even non-religious, practitioners of meditation or psychological

---

[3] *Asc.* II, 3, 3; III, 31, 8.

analysis who claim to find in St. John of the Cross an adequate
formulation of their own experience. The conclusion is that
the experience in each case is identical, and that therefore St.
John's mystical experience is simply an instance of the universal mystical way and has no intrinsic connection, other
than as from a random starting point, with Christian belief.
On the other hand, there are Christians devoted to the life of
prayer who find St. John's doctrine of dark faith singularly
lacking in, and even destructive of, the presence of Jesus Christ.
Abbot Columba Marmion, in a letter to a Carmelite nun
(1918), acknowledges: "I have read St. John of the Cross
attentively. His writings are not suited to my soul. They take
from me my liberty in my dealings with God. My inclination is
to find everything in Jesus and through Him. He is the 'Way'
which the Father has given us, it is by Him that we must go.
When I try to make my mental prayer in the 'void', putting
aside all the beautiful words, images and comparisons which
Jesus used in His teaching, I am paralysed". The presumption
here seems to be that in 'the void' of the dark night of faith
Jesus is no longer the Way through whom we must go. Under
this influence of Marmion, Abbot John Chapman also writes:
" . . . for fifteen years or so, I hated St. John of the Cross, and
called him a Buddhist. . . . Then I found I had wasted fifteen
years, so far as prayer was concerned".[4]

The problem has its source in St. John's cardinal affirmation that nothing that can be comprehended by man, nothing
that is an achieved part of his experience, can have any
immediate resemblance to God. To follow the divine call into
a more profound relationship of faith in prayer must therefore
involve the 'setting aside' of all particular images and concepts
in favour of a 'pure' and 'simple' loving attention. And even
particular conceptions of Christ himself fall within the sphere
of things which are to be transcended by pure faith:

---

[4](*The Spiritual Letters of Dom John Chapman*, ed. Hudleston, London, 1935.
Letter XCIII, p. 269). His developed hard contrast in this letter between St. Teresa
and St. John is, as he suspected, "simply exaggerating, and . . . I am all wrong. No
doubt I am. But I don't yet see *where* I am wrong". p. 273.

meditation is a discursive action wrought by means of images, forms and figures that are fashioned by the [interior] senses, as when we imagine Christ crucified or bound to the column, or at another of the stations.... All these imaginings must be cast out from the soul, which will remain in darkness, so that it may attain to divine union; for they cannot be a proximate means of union with God.

(*Asc.* II, 12, 3)

John allows that such meditation on the humanity of Christ is necessary for beginners in the way of prayer in order to enkindle their love for God by sensuous devotion. For as long as God does not inhibit such activity they must continue in it.[5] But in the ascent of the ladder of contemplation, when God does thus intervene, the soul must resolutely leave behind such lower rungs (*Asc.* II, 12, 5). It might therefore seem that the more profoundly contemplative the faith, the less determinately Christian it will be, that it becomes free of any particular mode of revelation and more purely an absolute reaching out of the human spirit for the Absolute hidden ground of being. Such was the kind of spiritual direction offered to St. Teresa at one stage of her life. She followed it willingly for a while, but then rejects it most vehemently. Certain directors

advise us earnestly to put aside all corporeal imagination and to approach the contemplation of the Divinity. And they say that anything else, even Christ's humanity, will hinder or impede those who have arrived so far from attaining to perfect contemplation.... O Lord of my soul and my God, Jesus Christ crucified. Never once do I recall this opinion which I held without a feeling of pain: I believe I was committing an act of high treason, though I committed it in ignorance.... I believe myself that this is the reason why many souls, after succeeding in experiencing the Prayer of Union, do not make further progress and achieve a very great spiritual freedom....[6]

[5] *Asc.* II, 13, 2 and 6; 15, 1; *D.N.* I, 9, 8.
[6] *Life*, Chap 22, c.f. also *Mansions*, VI, 7.

The terms in which she represents this pernicious advice appear to be disturbingly similar to those of the *Ascent* and the *Dark Night*. And yet while St. John was confessor to the Convent of the Incarnation (1572-1577) they shared frequently and profoundly in the things of the spirit, after which St. Teresa wrote appreciatively:

> He is a divine, heavenly man. I assure you, my daughter, since he left us I have not found another like him in the whole of Castile.... You would never believe how lonely I feel without him.... He is indeed the Father of my soul and one of those with whom it does me most good to converse.[7]

There is indeed a significant difference between them in temperament and the description of phenomena, but they are certainly not *"absolute opposites"* (Chapman, *op.cit*, XCIII) in their doctrine. In fact, as we shall now see, the full evidence of John's own writings indicates that his apophatic way of darkness is as wholly Christological as Teresa's mystical life, "of Jesus". At every moment of its development, even in its darkest contemplative form, faith is a "crystalline fount", the "faith of Christ my Spouse", "because it is from Christ" (*Cant.* 12:2f).

To begin with the more general context: the *Spiritual Canticle* traces the mystical ascent from its very beginnings to its consummation in Spiritual Marriage, and the whole dialogue is between the soul as Bride and the Spouse, identified clearly as Christ. It is a hymn of longing for God, but always with the recognition that it is the love of Christ which is the way into that life of God:

> It is as though she said, 'O Word, my Spouse, show me the place where you are hidden'; wherein she begs him to manifest his divine essence, for the place where the Son of God is hidden as St. John says, is 'the bosom of the Father'.
>
> (*Cant.* 1:3)

---

[7]Letter to M. Ana de Jesus, 1578; *Letters*, ed. E.A. Peers, no. 261.

We must understand here that St. John of the Cross is not offering this as some kind of remote, "merely doctrinal" gloss upon an experience of a nameless Absolute. Christ himself is essential to the inward contemplative intention of faith. The intensity of specific, personal relationship is unmistakable:

> The Word, the Son of God, together with the Father and the Holy Spirit, is hidden in essence and in presence in the inmost being of the soul. Therefore the soul that would find him ... must enter within itself in deepest recollection; ... there the good contemplative must seek him with love.
>
> (*Cant.* 1:6)

There is no distinction here between the faith of doctrine and that of prayer. His way of interiority is not presented as a discovery of inner realms of consciousness which are then allegorized or symbolized in speculative allusions to Christ. Directly and practically, by contemplative faith, we seek "him".

But in what sense can this be true when, in the formless experience, there is no clear determination of the object of faith as Christ? The very question implies a conceptualist misunderstanding of what it means to know a person. John insists that even when particular images and ideas of Christ are genuinely suspended by God and willingly foregone by the soul, the reaching out of loving faith towards the same person is not at all diminished. For the conceptual darkness, being passively undergone, is *with respect to* a previously vivid commitment of imagination, mind and heart to Jesus. The deprivation is experienced as a deprivation of him; or rather, of particular concepts about him:

> 'Behold, the affliction of love is not cured save by thy presence and thy form'.... The soul feels herself to have the shadow of love, which is the affliction whereof she here speaks, desiring that it may be perfectly formed by means of the Form to whom the shadow belongs, which is her Spouse, the Word, the Son of God who, as St. Paul says, is the brightness of his glory and the figure of his substance.
>
> (*Cant.* 11:12)

And so, in the darkness of contemplative faith the soul is even more deeply convinced that it is Christ, now more painfully "hidden", who is the object of her consuming desire. Though without a clearly defined object, the contemplative's 'meaning' is intensely and consciously informed with the presence of Christ.

And so the darkness of contemplative faith is no mindless vacuity. The deprivation of specific notions of Christ is only in favour of an even truer mode of knowledge of him—and that means, of a more complete identification with him:

> if the impediments and veils [of creaturely forms] were completely removed, the soul would then find itself in a condition of pure detachment and poverty of spirit and, being simple and pure, would be transformed into simple and pure Wisdom, which is the Son of God.
>
> (*Asc.* II, 15, 4)

The formlessness in the intellect is caused by the transcendent brightness of divine light—a far more perfect apprehension of God's Personal Wisdom than any image or concept about it. Thus, although passivity here signifies not only the experienced infusion of God's grace, but also a certain intellectual indeterminacy, this latter is in fact the sign of a positive transformation into the likeness of God's Word.

But there still remains the crucial question of the role of Jesus Christ in contemplative faith. The formlessness and simplicity may well be an image of divine Wisdom, the eternal Word, but how does it relate to the historically determined Incarnate Word? Standing at the head of the discourse on dark faith, as its perfect source of meaning, is the total desolation of Christ on the Cross:

> solid and perfect spirituality consists in the annihilation of all sweetness in God, in aridity, distaste and trial, which is the true spiritual Cross and the detachment of the spiritual poverty of Christ.
>
> (*Asc.* II, 7, 5)

Just as, positively, the unrestricted quality of pure faith corresponds to the incomprehensible fullness of the divine Word, so also, in its negative aspect of intellectual desolation, it is an "imitation of Christ, who is the Way, the Truth and the Life" (Jn 14:6; *Asc.* II, 7, 8). Moreover, that imitation is not just the copying of a remote model, but a consent to be taken up into the mystery of Christ's death:

> at the moment of his death he was likewise annihilated in his soul and was deprived of any relief and consolation, since his Father left him in the most intense aridity.... Wherefore he had to cry out, saying, 'My God, my God, why hast thou forsaken me?'.... The truly spiritual man may understand the mystery of the gate and of the way of Christ and so become united with God, and may know that the more completely he is annihilated for God's sake, the more completely he is united to God and the greater the work he accomplishes.
>
> (*Asc.* II, 7, 11)

It is precisely the agonizing inability to grasp any conception of Jesus or of his Father as an illuminating object of meditative prayer which constitutes the truest experience of faith 'in the Passion of Christ'—that is, subjectively, from within the redemptive mystery of his own God-forsakenness. It is faith *as* the Passion of Christ.

Turning now to "the golden substance", the object of faith: the further we follow St. John's reflections on faith, the more we see that its span is virtually limitless. It is an intrinsic 'created' reality in the believer's life—"the consent of the soul", "a habit of the soul, certain and obscure"—and yet it reaches "immediately" to God himself and is "proportionate" to the infinity and incomprehensibility of the divine nature (*Asc.* II, 1, 1; 9, 1). This is the key to understanding authentic activity and passivity in the spiritual life: the energy and richness of the new creation is to be integrated in a single mystery with the 'nothingness' of spiritual poverty and receptivity. For even in the most complete union, precisely because it is a union of love, the soul must remain other than the Beloved from whom all its riches flow (*Cant.* 30: 1; *L.F.* 2:34). And so, when St. John speaks of faith as the "means" to that union with God, it is not as the physical way to an end must be separate from that end. Faith is itself a real mediation of God; it is an essential part of the mystery of man becoming deiform.

> So, faith gives and communicates to us God himself, but covered with the silver of faith; but it fails not for that reason to give him to us in truth, even as one may give a silvered vessel, which is also a vessel of gold, for, though covered with silver, it is nonetheless a golden vessel that he gives.
>
> (*Cant.* 12:4)

The conceptual truths which the believer receives in the formulated articles of the Creed are signs of divine realities of grace, which really condition his existence. The preached word of faith is a sacrament of the Word, because the silver surface of the propositions is not only a concealment, but also a certain assurance, of the divine reality which they mediate.

Such spatial metaphors of outward and inward, frequently borrowed from the Bible, are the most common way John has of treating the nature of faith. God is concealed in a tabernacle of dark waters; enclosed within a dark cloud, he came to fill the Temple, to meet Moses on Sinai, to speak with Job (*Asc.* II, 9, 3). As with Gideon's soldiers, the lamps of divine light are concealed within the pitchers of this mortal life of faith; the glory of vision will shine out when they are broken (*Ibid*). Interpreting the promise in Isaiah, "I will give you the hidden treasures and I will reveal to you the substance and mysteries of the secrets" (Is 45:3), John observes that

> this substance of the secrets is God himself, for God is the substance of faith and its conception, and faith is the secret and the mystery.
>
> (*Cant.* 1:10)

Such reliance upon imagery precludes a high degree of intellectual precision. However, its allusiveness has the great advantage of embracing a far richer spectrum of religious experience than a precise systematic method could do. Thus, it is very important to recognize that in these images John is trying to express symbolically not only an abstract and universal notion of faith, but also the concrete experience of that virtue. The spatial imagery reflects not just the levels of ontological reality, but also the different reaches of the contemplative's own experience where these realities are discerned. "For beneath this darkness the understanding is united with God" (*Asc.* II, 9, 1)—that is meant to be an evocation of the complex structure of contemplative faith, with its experiential 'feeling' for the different reaches of the depths of the soul. Firstly, on the conceptual 'cataphatic' level of credal formulation, faith can make affirmations of God's infinity, of his Unity and Trinity, etc. (*Asc.* II, 9, 1). But that affirmation is one of believing, not seeing: it proceeds out of the *darkness* of faith, "which blinds and dazzles the understanding" (*Ibid*). And yet that darkness does not denote a realm which is totally inaccessible, as though the reaches of understanding were totally exhausted and delimited by the merely conceptual. Made strong by faith as a new power, the mind retains a certain but obscure understanding of divine things "beneath this darkness". That gaze of faith recognizes the unseen reaches to be authentic mystery, that is, charged with divine meaning. There, "in my inmost parts" (*en mis entrañas*), the soul is united with God, and perceives itself to be progressively shaped by him, restored to the true personal being of self-possession by being restored in his image:

> it is like a stone that is approaching ever nearer to its centre. Or again, it feels like the wax that has begun to receive the impression of the seal and has not perfectly received its form. Again, it knows itself to be like the image of a first sketch and outline, and cries out to him who outlined it that he complete its painting and formation.
>
> (*Cant.* 12:1)

All that the soul can do, then, is to beg that God go forward with his work of perfecting his image in her. It may seem poor, but that profound desire is itself her effective cooperation with the divine work, the perfecting of her spiritual receptivity.

Thus faith heads towards a "substantial" contact between God and the soul.[8] But if it is so powerfully efficacious, creative of the divine image, then its source can only be God Himself. That is the meaning of a beautiful change in the metaphor of contemplative "gazing" which occurs in the *Canticle*. In the earlier stanzas one to thirteen, leading up to the Spiritual Betrothal, it is the soul who is searching out her Beloved, contemplating his traces in the beauty of creation and asking that he reveal his presence so that she might see him in open vision. But as soon as that quest begins to be fulfilled in an eminent degree, it is God himself who becomes the great Contemplative. We have seen how the divine glance bestows on all creation its natural goodness and beauty. Here, in the strength and grace bestowed by God's loving attentiveness, the soul is empowered to return its own gaze of loving faith:

> When you did look upon me,
> Your eyes imprinted in me their grace;
> For this cause did you love me greatly,
> And in this did my eyes deserve to adore
> That which they saw in you.

(st. 32)

> ... God, by means of his charity, might form faith in her, which is her eye.

(para. 5)

Because all of its energy is directed into the abyss of God, contemplative faith can seem to be utterly useless, like the woman's ointment "wasted" on the feet of Jesus. It cannot add to the glory of the always transcendent God, and yet it is a truly 'meritorious work', manifesting an already achieved transformation in grace and winning still more:

---

[8] *Cant.* 19:4; 26:5, 30:1; *L.F.* 2:8; 2:21.

through this grace and worth which she has received of him she has merited his love, and has now in herself become worthy to adore her Beloved pleasingly and to do works worthy of his grace and love.[9]

Such is the gravitation which draws the soul ever more swiftly and profoundly into its deepest centre where God dwells—"namely, that God gives grace for grace"—(*Cant.* 33:7; 32:5; Jn 1:16). Therefore, there is nothing of value in the soul which is not an effect of God's loving gratuitous gift; which in turn means that at the *origin* of all his work of supernatural beauty in the soul there was a moment when she could offer nothing but swarthiness, *color moreno*, "the deformity and blackness of faults and imperfections and the baseness of my natural condition" (*Cant.* 33:5). Therefore, while the beauty of her adoration is truly her own, it is still wholly the gift of his recreative gaze upon her.

Faith, then, in its origin, growth and perfection is a principle of pure transcendence, wholly from God and wholly toward him. And yet therein lies its richness for the soul. While the power and the purity of contemplative faith is measured by the extent to which it is turned away from self in adoration and total fascination with the Beloved, its effect is to perfect the contemplative in divine grace and beauty. Why? Because that selfless mystical gazing is but a slight reflection of the recreative gaze of God.

> By the eyes of the Spouse is here understood His merciful Divinity which, bending down in mercy to the soul, imprints and infuses in her His love and grace, thereby beautifying her and raising her up to make her consort of His very Divinity.
>
> (*Cant.* 32:4)

---

[9]*Cant.* 32:2. " . . . for the soul to be able to gaze upon God is to perform works in the grace of God, and so the powers of the soul have merit in adoration because they have adored in the grace of their God wherein all operation is meritorious" (*Cant.* 32:8).

Finally, we complete our discussion of faith by returning to its most central association of darkness. Because the original glory of faith lies in God's beholding of the soul rather than in the latter's own subjective act, we might understand why the contemplative's experience of faith should not be one of radiant light. Contemplative faith is a transcending not only of natural knowledge but also beyond itself. Even as it is realized as an attained virtue and a supernatural experience, it demands of its own nature that it be left behind in a reaching out towards the gold beneath the silver, the painting beyond the sketch. Consequently, the thirst for self-transcendence becomes ever more implacable as the soul enters more deeply into faith. Herein lies the essence of the Dark Night in all its purifying rigor of the passive night of spirit:

> The reason that the soul suffers so much at this time is that the nearer it comes to union with God, the more keenly it feels within itself its emptiness of God and the direst darkness, together with spiritual fire which dries and purges it ... until God draws it into his Divine brightness through transformation of love.
>
> (*Cant.* 13:1)

Following St. John's conception of the virtues, the 'brightness' toward which dark faith heads in this life will most fittingly be treated under the heading of love.

Hope

This dark night of faith is a spiritual ascent which is completed in a union of love. But the virtue which most closely coincides in St. John's doctrine with the very movement towards that goal is hope. We have insisted on the penetrating, transcending quality of contemplative faith: but in spite of the many sensuous and affective associations that John gives it, it remains a predominantly intellectual dynamism and is most clearly manifest in the act of prayer. The virtue of hope seems to extend that dynamism beyond the power of contemplative gazing to a more rounded engagement of the whole of Christian living. It is not just a matter of the soul's gaze of faith penetrating the divine mystery. The soul herself goes forward to union. "Hope is the virtue of progress in the spiritual life".[10] The threefold disguise which veils the Lover's escape to God exemplifies this truth: an inner garment of brilliant white, signifying the purity of faith; an outer one of red, that is, of fervent and passionate love (*con ansias en amores enflamada*) binding everything together; and between these a green vestment of hope, whose colour represents the freshness and surging vitality (*viveza y animosidad y levantamiento*) of growth in the spiritual life (*D.N.* II, 21). Being so closely involved with movement, hope has a crucial role to play in authentic initiative and passivity.[11]

Because hope is the virtue by which the grace of God sanctifies the 'memory', it would be well to make some brief comment on the nature of that faculty as understood by St. John: the nature of memory will determine to some extent the mode of its sanctification.[12] Most striking, perhaps, is that aspect of memory and hope which could be seen either as its peculiar wholeness or else as its ambiguity. In the garments of disguise, hope lies between faith and love; that is also the order of the general exposition of the active night of spirit in *The Ascent of*

---

[10]Marie-Eugene, *I Am a Daughter of the Church*, Cork, 1955, p. 380.

[11]"Mystical asceticism, the perfect response of genuine love, is always a delicate art. It must move strongly between that proud activism that believes in its own power and thus checks the expansion and the initiatives of God's love for the soul, and that selfish and lazy quietism that fixates the soul's love for its God in the immobility of tepidity or death. Mystical asceticism finds its measure and its expression in the practice of the virtue of hope'. Marie-Eugene, *op.cit*, pp 378f.

[12]In holding memory to be a third spiritual faculty along with intellect and will, John departs from the Thomist tradition which recognizes no other spiritual functions than the apprehensive or cognitive (intellect) and the appetitive or conative (will). One could invoke the authority of St. Augustine for the distinction of the memory. (c.f. *Confess*, X, 8-16. E. Gilson, *The Christian Philosophy of Saint Augustine*, trans. L. Lynch, London, 1961, pp 66-105). But St. John does not trouble to do so; further evidence as to how lightly he stood regarding the traditions of philosophical psychology—loose and uncritical, or pragmatic and flexible, depending on one's point of view. For detailed discussions on this area of his psychology c.f. Andre Bord, *Memoire et esperance chez Jean de la Croix*, Paris, 1971.

Mount Carmel—faith purifies the intellect (*Asc.* II); hope, the memory (*Asc.* III, 1-15); and love, the will (*Asc.* III, 16-45). It is not improbable to take this pattern as an indication that the 'memory' for St. John spans both cognitive and affective dimensions. The cognitive is powerfully suggested by his elaboration of the image of hope as the "helmet of salvation" (c.f., I Thess 5:8): it has a visor

> which the soul is permitted to use so that its eyes may look upwards, but nowhere else; for this is the function which hope habitually performs in the soul, namely, the directing of its eyes upwards to look at God alone.
>
> (*D.N.* II, 21, 7)

This language of the exclusive gaze towards God coincides exactly with that used of faith: hope in the memory would seem to include a certain intellectual intention. At the same time, there is a strong appetitive and affective stream. The gaze upon God is an *expectant* gaze, it gives the soul "ardour and courage and aspiration for the things of eternal life" (*loc. cit.* para. 6), it is a matter of "setting the heart upon God" and of finding "pleasure" in nothing but him (para. 8). The memory strengthened by hope appears also to be a faculty of ardent desire.

But if hope thus includes both cognitive and affective elements, it is not simply to be identified with either. That which is really proper to memory is the function of possession—we might even say, in a peculiar sense, of self-possession. For "together with the fancy" it is the "archive or storehouse" of all one's past experience—of sense and spirit,[13] of knowing and of loving, both natural and supernatural (*Asc.* II, 16, 2; III, 7, 1: 14, 1). It is thus a receptive and a virtually limitless capacity in which is present subliminally the whole of one's past history, and which is open as a passive potentiality towards all future experience. As the store of concrete, indi-

---

[13]John would refer sensuous images to *fantasia* and spiritual forms to the 'memory' in a strict sense (c.f. *Asc.* III, 14, 1).

vidual, non-transferable experience, it belongs to the subject in
an absolutely unique way. In fact it constitutes an aspect of his
very being, for it is the radical, factual presence to self of all
that his unique personal life has made of him. It is not the
same as the more common notion of self-possession; this latter
refers to a more highly differentiated condition of personal
awareness, of an equanimity which is achieved through deliberate rational detachment from one's immediate flow of
experience. Memory is simply the accumulation of that 'first-
level' factual stream, the passive or receptive capacity of the
person undergoing the fabric of his life.

Besides this passive capacity, memory also has an active
power of recall, the summoning into conscious awareness of
past events and the imaginative construction of past and future
possibles—'what might have been', 'what could be'. Now, for
the purposes of ascetical life, especially in the exercise of theological hope, it is very important to distinguish two different
modes of experiencing this power of remembrance. One is
deliberate, in which the soul feels itself to have command:

> Now, after the soul has had experience of one of these
> apprehensions, it can recall it whenever it will (*cuando
> quisiere*).
>
> (*Asc.* III, 14, 1)

Although determined by the forms of past personal experience, this is clearly an 'active' exercise in the fullest sense—a
free, deliberate calling to mind of that experience.[14] On the
other hand, memory's actuation can be quite spontaneous.
The subject can feel himself to be passive, subject to his own
'faculty' which seems to have a life of its own—hence the play
of undesired temptations and distractions, when memory will
throw into consciousness "many and various forms of the
imagination" and the associated sensuous arousal of "movements and desires" (*Cant.* 16:4). Such persistent assaults often

---

[14]As we shall soon demonstrate, however, John strongly denies that this deliber-
ateness is an assurance of authentic freedom. It is the function of hope to liberate this
free *power* into a new, grace-formed *condition* of the freedom of the children of God.

cannot be prevented by the most fervent efforts. This lack of integrity is very apparent when St. John, with considerable psychological insight, observes that it is precisely fear and anxious reluctance which can heighten a person's helplessness in the face of distressing sexual fantasies:

> The third source whence these impure motions are apt to proceed in order to make war upon the soul is often the fear which such persons have conceived for these impure represen-tations and motions. Something that they see or say or think brings them to mind, so that they suffer them through no fault of their own.
>
> (*D.N.* I, 4, 4)

It seems that, inasmuch as memory is a 'spiritual faculty', it has that much more native power of its own, and so its disordered intrusions arising from man's fallen condition are all the less amenable to rational control.

Turning now to the virtue of hope: in common with the other theological virtues, it appears predominantly as a reversal of the natural power.[15] Possession is drastically reshaped to dispossession. Memory's passive power of receiving and con-taining takes a negative experiential form of a great void and emptiness; and its active power of recall becomes, paradox-ically, a power of "forgetfulness" (*Asc.* III, 9, 4).

> Of all these forms and kinds of knowledge the soul must strip and void itself ... it must remain barren and bare, as if these forms had never passed through it, and in total oblivion and suspension. And this cannot happen unless the memory be annihilated as to all its forms, if it is to be united with God.
>
> (*Asc.* III, 2, 4)

---

[15]All that we have said above (pp 99-118) about 'emptiness' is particularly apposite to this discussion of hope.

And why embark upon such a fearful programme of negation? For much the same reason that faith has to "empty" the understanding:

> For [union] cannot happen except by total separation from all forms which are not God; for God falls beneath no definite form or kind of knowledge whatsoever.
>
> (*Ibid.* c.f. also *Asc.* III, 5, 3)

This we might call the basic apophatic condition. Union with God who is of his nature incomprehensible cannot be reached unless the memory "rise above itself—that is, above all distinct knowledge and apprehensible possessions" (*Asc.* III, 2, 3).

The notion of "possession" extends the emptying function of hope to a more practical, ascetical realm. The remembrance of past events and the calling to mind of possible future things may, as we have seen, be quite deliberate and in this real sense 'free'. Nevertheless, inasmuch as the power of remembrance is not purified by the grace of God, then, in spite of all its voluntary nature, it manifests an even deeper bondage. For the good natural function of memory to possess is vitiated by a dominating proprietary spirit, distorting it into a destructive 'possessiveness'. The power to contain and to recall experience topples over into an exaggerated, activist grasping. And because it grasps at the riches of one's own personal experience, real or imagined, it must be essentially solepsistic, turning one back upon his own history and thus hindering him from the passing beyond self which is his true mode of personal being. Deliberate "resting in" the treasures of memory is voluntary indeed, but its consent is to bondage. For this reason, John so often speaks of the emptying of memory by hope as a liberation:

> they should seek to forget [past extraordinary experiences of prayer] in order that they may be free.
>
> (*Asc.* III, 9, 4; c.f. also, III, 13, 1)

This ascetic discipline is not a diminishment but an expansion of the memory's true power,

drawing it out from its natural state and limitations and
raising it above itself.

(*Asc.* III, 2, 3)

Spiritual poverty leaves the memory free and disencumbered
(*libre y desembarazada*) of the past and of oneself (*Asc.* III, 2,
14). Holiness of life includes a sublime unself-consciousness or
self-forgetfulness.

It is clear also that this freedom belongs not merely to a
distant, abstract state of life, the end result of ascesis. The
exercise of hope is itself the discovery and the expression of
this new liberty, and John uses strong language to convey the
vigour of the active night of spiritual hope. Those who wish to
progress in contemplation must "seek to forget" past favours
(*las procuren olvidar, Asc.* III, 9, 4). The soul

> must proceed by denying and refusing to the uttermost
> whatever it is able to deny of what it has apprehended,
> whether natural or supernatural.
>
> (*Asc.* III, 2, 3)

While admitting that perfection comes only as a gift of God,
John insists that the soul must do all in its power to prepare
for that gift: without any extraordinary intervention of God,
but simply by one's own grace-supported power, 'actively', one
can exercise hope as renunciation and a power of forgetfulness.[16] And yet for all its fierce resolution, this active ascesis of
hope must avoid being distorted into presumptuous over-
reaching. In some beautifully balanced phrases, St. John
captures the subtlety of contemplative hope, which must be a
resolution simply to 'let go' as much as to suppress:

> ... he must allow himself to forget [these perceptions]
> immediately (*las deje luego olvidar*), and to do so with the

---

[16]'The truth, I repeat, is that God must place the soul in this supernatural state of
perfection; but the soul, as far as in it lies, must be continually preparing itself; and
this it can do by natural means, especially with the help that God is continually giving
it' (*Asc.* III, 2, 13).

same efficacy, if it is necessary, as that with which others
remember.

(*Asc.* III, 2, 14)

The higher freedom of hope turns the raw edge of voluntarism
into the less anxious zeal of detachment—"freely allowing the
memory to fall into forgetfulness (*dejàndola libremente perder
en olvido*)" (*Asc.* III, 2, 14).

Before proceeding to the more passively infused experience
of hope, we must add a precision regarding deliberate 'forgetfulness'. It is most definitely a *moral* exercise. It is directed not
so much against the mere presence in consciousness of things
remembered, but at the acquisitive spirit with which they are
summoned and grasped. In order to mortify that vice, the soul
must deny itself the indulgent, self-complacent recalling of
experience. But insofar as they arise spontaneously, the discipline will be in terms of setting *value* upon them—"to pay no
heed to them" (*de ninguna ha de hacer caso*) (*Asc.* III, 13, 1).
Furthermore, when the true goal of spiritual gifts is recognized, they may be deliberately remembered without any
offence against hope:

> these apprehensions may be recalled when they produce
> good effects, not that they may be dwelt upon, but they
> may quicken the soul's knowledge and love of God.
>
> (*Asc.* III, 14, 2)

St. John might be uncompromising in his demands, but he is
not fanatical. The vice of possessiveness must be utterly purged
away by 'forgetfulness', but there is one possession that he
values supremely, and memory may be enlisted for its growth:

> let the soul endeavour to pay heed only to the possession of
> the love of God which [graces in prayer] cause within it. . . .
> And with this sole end in view it may at times recall that
> image and apprehension caused it by love, in order to set
> the spirit on its course of love.
>
> (*Asc.* III, 13, 6)

In such a case, memory is not trapped within the limits of

personal history, but has attained its proper function of growth and self-transcendence.

If hope is the virtue of progress in the spiritual life, hope itself must grow ever deeper. And in this regard it is most important to recall that it is a *supernatural* virtue, reaching directly towards God and infused by him. Therefore its increase is only secondarily dependent upon the soul's summoning up ever deeper resources of resolution and desire. It arises ultimately from the gift of God by which these resources are transformed. And so, with the passive night of spirit a new mode of hope begins, when that divine assistance becomes the experientially dominant factor.[17] And not, as we have seen, that the soul in the midst of the affliction of that Night recognizes it as a blessing. The original expectancy and desire become still more intense, indeed, excruciatingly so. But now, instead of a sense of swift light movement towards God and a purposeful casting aside of all that might hinder union, the soul feels itself to be fearfully borne down by an immense dark load:

> its clear perception, as it thinks, that God has abandoned it and, in his abhorrence of it, has flung it into darkness.
>
> (*D.N.* II, 6, 2)

There is no question of taking any new initiative towards God. Every step is prevented by the assailing divine Wisdom, the soul is oppressed with the weight of his greatness (*D.N.* II, 5, 6; Job 23:6), shut in by the bars of the earth, the bonds of its sin (*D.N.* II, 6, 3; Jonas 2:6).

> Then hope cannot but groan and sigh ardently and in silence ... it seems almost passive, with the energies of its restrained dynamism concentrated in its gaze and desires.[18]

---

[17] St. John does not devote an explicit section to a 'passive night of hope'; but the implications for memory are clear enough in Book II of the *Dark Night*.

[18] Marie-Eugene, *op. cit.*, p 380.

This is where the vast motive power of hope is concentrated in pure expectancy. There is nothing to be done except willingly to undergo God's work:

> it behoves the soul to endure much (*mucho conviene pasar*) and to suffer with patience and hope.
> (*Asc.* III, 2, 15)

The reversal seems to be complete. The soul cannot see itself "going forth" as it did in the beginning of its quest for God, and yet, paradoxically, in its constriction and helplessness it is now more spiritually powerful. That pure expectancy wounds the heart of God, "since that which moves and conquers is the importunity of hope" (*D.N.* II, 21, 8; c.f. *Songs*, 4:9). It is only in this context of radical passive purification that St. John alludes to the kind of extraordinary phenomena in which forgetfulness means not only a moral detachment but a loss of awareness with respect to the mundane fabric of life:

> for occasionally, when God brings about these touches of union in the memory, . . . it is emptied and purged of all kinds of knowledge. It remains in great oblivion—at times in complete oblivion—so that it has to put forth a great effort and to labour greatly in order to remember anything.
> (*Asc.* III, 2, 5)

Including such things as insensitivity to physical pain (para. 6), these phenomena reflect the popular caricature of 'the mystic': but John spends only a few paragraphs on them (*Asc.* III, 2, 5-12), assuring us that the passivity of suspended consciousness is only accidental to the real work of purification and that, far from being a spiritual ideal, it belongs to those not yet in perfect union with God (para. 6).

Hope is certainly 'forward-looking'. But it should be apparent by now that the reversal which it effects in the memory is not primarily a temporal change, as though the soul's concern should be drawn from past experience to that of the future. A man can be just as surely imprisoned in wishful thinking about future possessions as in futile reliving of the past. The reversal is rather a shift of one's deepest concern to the transcendent, from a clutching at any particular goods, past or future, to a pure expectancy for the absolute Good. When John invokes the authority of St. Paul, "Now hope that is seen is not hope. For who hopes for what he sees?" (Rom 8:24), he interprets the 'seeing' as possession:

> for hope always relates to that which is not possessed; for if it were possessed there would be no hope.
>
> (*Asc.* II, 6, 3)

But the poverty that he speaks of is not merely with respect to future things that might yet be grasped. Taking up the same text again, he insists, more strongly, that hope "withdraws the memory from that which it is *capable* of possessing (*se puede poseer*)" (*D.N.* II, 21, 11). The dispossession must be unconditional. Hope must be "in God alone", in God who is "incomprehensible" and therefore beyond the memory's "power of possessing" (*Asc.* III, 2, 3). It draws the soul not so much from past to future, as towards an eternal present. And so the same principle of utter transcendence is operative in hope as in faith: it must not be an anticipation even of 'union with God' in the sense of a sublime experience yet to be enjoyed, for, as experience, that union is possessed, and hope will have the soul reach beyond even his greatest gifts towards God himself.

> For the soul is so completely emptied of every possession and support that it fixes its eyes and its care upon nothing but God, putting its mouth in the dust if so there might be hope.
>
> (*D.N.* II, 21, 9; Lam 3:29)

This consuming drive into a mystery at once incomprehensible and totally personal can have one end for the soul—no more to possess, but to be wholly possessed by God:

> Wherefore the functions of the memory and the other faculties in this state are all divine; for, when at last God

possesses the faculties and has become the entire master of them through their entire transformation in himself, it is he himself who moves and commands them divinely, according to his divine Spirit and will.

(*Asc.* III, 2, 8)

The way of spiritual poverty therefore issues in glorious riches, for to be thus seized by God's power means to share in his sovereign freedom over created things. No longer do they touch man as an alternative to God, as his spiritual enemy "the world" (*D.N.* II, 21, 6). Their finitude and contingency is no seed of diminishment for the soul, because they are now experienced "in their truth" (*Asc.* III, 20, 2f), that is, in their pure relationship to God.

> Mine are the heavens and mine is the earth; mine are the peoples, the righteous are mine and mine are the sinners; the angels are mine and the Mother of God and all things are mine; and God Himself is mine and for me, for Christ is mine and all for me. What, then, do you ask for and seek, my soul? Yours is all this, and it is all for you.
>
> (*Sayings* 25)

This "prayer of the soul enkindled with love" is St. John's own *Magnificat* Canticle. He learnt it from the perfect disciple, the perfect model of God's own poor, the one who perfectly received and gave back all:

> the most glorious Virgin Our Lady, who, being raised to this high estate from the beginning, had never the form of any creature imprinted in her soul, nor was she moved by such, but was invariably guided by the Holy Spirit.
>
> (*Asc.* III, 2, 10)

Love

VITAL PERFECTION

Love is the perfection of the spiritual life. If the soul's ascent follows the way of the dispossession of hope through the luminous darkness of faith, its consummation is reached especially in the third theological virtue:

> the end and aspiration which the soul had so much desired, ... the union of love.
>
> (*D.N.* II, 21, 12)

From the very outset the goal has been conceived thus, coloring all that happens on the way. All the manifold forms of the dark night are but designs of God's Wisdom purifying and strengthening the soul for "the perfect union of the love of God" (*Asc.* Prol, 1; *D.N.* I, 1; II, 18, 4). Therefore, besides recognizing that the dark gaze of faith reaches towards beatific vision, and the spiritual poverty of hope to the possession of the glory of God, we can also understand these two virtues as each finding their perfection in charity. Its splendid scarlet vestment is thrown over the white and green of the others to complete the soul's disguise:

> it even gives value to the other virtues, bestowing on them vigour and strength to protect the soul, and grace and beauty to please the Beloved with them, for without charity no virtue has grace before God.
>
> (*D.N.* II, 21, 10)

Again, it is possible to discern such a progression of love in St. John's three major poems and their commentaries. They are all passionate love songs, but there is a certain distinct predominating tone in each: firstly, the celebration of the blessed night of faith, '*En una noche oscura*'; then the hope which drives the long quest of the Canticle, '*Adonde te escondiste, Amado*'; and finally, the yearning and afflictive love which animates both of these bursts out clearly and strongly in '*Llama de amor viva*'. In a profoundly evangelical vision St. John sees the ultimate meaning of human life as lying only here. The refined value of all things can be reduced to one criterion: "At eventide they will examine thee in love" (*Sayings*, 59).

In this respect, then, love is unique. It differs even from faith and hope, for their very nature appears to be entirely self-transcending, while love includes its own element of genuine attainment and rest. As we have observed in the previous section, the quality of hope's self-emptying can be judged, paradoxically, by the 'possession' of the love of God; the only thing that survives the ruthless apophatic denial of faith and hope is the love to which they minister and which preserves and animates them. Nevertheless, the perfection of love must also be a *progressive* perfection. The movement towards God is by a secret ladder of contemplation of which every step, from first to last, is a certain degree of love:

> [contemplation] is an infused and loving knowledge of God which enlightens the soul and at the same time enkindles it with love, until it is raised up step by step even to God its Creator: for it is love alone which unites and joins the soul with God.
>
> (*D.N.* II, 18, 5)

St. John therefore holds together two features of love in vital tension. It is the essence of spiritual perfection—"the state of perfection, which consists in the perfect love of God" (*D.N.* II, 18, 4)—but at the same time it admits of an infinite range of quality and so is always open to growth. Indeed, the whole purpose of the *Living Flame* is to illustrate how, even in "the most perfect degree of perfection which may be attained in this life [and] ... beyond which a soul cannot pass", there still remains the immediate possibility that "the soul may become more completely perfected and grounded in love" (*L.F.* Prol, 3). A log completely penetrated by fire becomes one living flame: so, "love is never idle, but is continually in movement" (*L.F.* 1:8). For this reason there can be no surfeit of love; while it is the "centring" of the soul in God, it never blocks the drive towards its own increase:

> love is the inclination of the soul and the strength and power which it has to go to God, for, by means of love, the

soul is united with God; and thus, the more degrees of love
the soul has, the more profoundly does it enter into God
and the more it is centred in him.

(*L.F.* 1:13)

It is no coincidence that this meaning of love as a vital union is
similar to St. John the Evangelist speaking of the only Son as
eis ton kolpon tou patrou, "into the bosom of the Father" (Jn
1:18), with its sense of perfect movement or living presence.

This quality of love as inclination, strength and power
suggests that there is no more radical spring beneath love
which drives it onwards. Perhaps its greatest perfection is that
it contains its own source of further life. Unlike faith and
hope, love is not required to 'deny' itself in anticipation of a
totally other fullness, because its unitive function in no way
inhibits its self-transcendence. On the contrary, love is the
source of its own vigour:

> otherwise [the soul's] love would not be true; for the wages
> and recompense of love are nothing else, nor can the soul
> desire anything else, than greater love, until it attains to
> perfection of love; for love confers no payment except of
> itself.

(*Cant.* 9:7)

St. John's conception of love here draws very close to St.
Augustine's *pondus meum amor meus*, "My gravity is my
love" (*Confessions*, XIII, 10). Just as the gravity of a stone
belongs to its very nature, so love

> yet has power and force and inclination to descend and to
> attain this farthest and deepest centre.

(*L.F.* 1:11, c.f. also *Cant.* 11:1; 17:1)

Or like another irrepressible elemental movement,

> love is like fire, which ever rises upward with the desire to
> be absorbed in the centre of its sphere,

(*D.N.* II, 20, 6)

Love's demand to transcend all finite experience is just as
radical as that of faith and hope:

> the will can taste no pleasure and sweetness that bears any
> resemblance to that which is God.
>
> (*Asc.* II, 8, 5)

but in moving beyond every attained experience of love 'for
God's sake', the soul is only being true to the essential meaning
of that experience:

> for to love is to labour to detach and strip itself for God's
> sake of all that is not God.
>
> (*Asc.* II, 5, 7)

Considering this boundless fruitfulness of love and at the same
time the utter indigence of man, it is clear that the soul's
genuine love of God must be wholly received. There is no way
that a creature, totally dependent for its very being on God's
continuous creative act, could find in itself the source of such
endless vitality. The primary meaning of 'the love of God'
must always be that of the subjective genitive: not merely the
soul's love for God, but that same love as belonging to Him,
because it could derive only from Him. The reason why there
is no deeper fount of love than Love itself, is that God Himself
is that source. Thus God is always "the principal agent in this
matter":

> first, it must be known that, if a soul is seeking God, its
> Beloved is seeking it much more.
>
> (*L.F.* 3:28)

The priority of God's love is absolute, but it becomes fully
effective only when it is recognized by the soul and thus elicits
her personal response to that original gratuitous gift:

> knowing on the one hand the great debt she owes to God in
> that he has created her for himself alone, for which she

> owes him the service of her whole life, and in that he has
> redeemed her for himself alone, for which she owes him all
> the rest of the love of her will and the return of his love to
> her.
>
> (*Cant.* 1:1)

Therefore the exclusiveness of charity "for God alone" manifests a finality which God has stamped in the soul's very
existence: "he has created her for himself alone, ... he has
redeemed her for himself alone". The conscious motive of
charity in the spiritual life is not of the soul's own making, but
is rather a discovery, a personal appropriation, of the divine
initiative of love which is guiding the real order of things.

In this context St. John returns to the notion of God as the
original Contemplative whose gaze awakens the soul into her
own contemplative response. "For God to gaze is for him to
love" (*Cant.* 31:8); and when he beholds one single hair flut-
tering on the neck, that is, the charity with which all other
virtues are interwoven, He is captivated even further, "so great
is the love of God for strong love" (*Cant.* 31:4). Therefore, like
faith, love also has its sublime escalation as God gives grace
upon grace and invests still more of his creative love into the
relationship built upon that gift.

POWER

That allusion to "strong love" (*el amor fuerte*) reveals a very
important dimensionof St. John's spirituality. Commonly
speaking, to combine notions of love and passivity would
easily give rise to an ethos of vapid emotion, of nothing more
than a pseudo-mystical languor. But it should already be clear
that St. John's conception is moving in quite the opposite
direction. Although he by no means ignores the delicacy and
the tenderness of love,[19] a still more frequent association is its
power, its vehemence, even its violence:

---

[19]C.f. *D.N.* II, 13; *Cant.* 14ff; *L.F.* 1:17; passim.

'Break the web of this swift encounter'; ... because love
delights in the force of love and in forceful and impetuous
touches.

(*L.F.* 1:33)

Call to mind the turbulent energy of a Spanish baroque
reredos: the ascending swirls of gold and enamel form the
visual background to the great act of Incarnate divine love in
the passion of Jesus celebrated on the altar. That same energy
also marks St. John's contemplative experience of love. The
meaning of the soul's 'passivity' in love, as we have seen, is
simply its 'being subject to love'. Therefore, that divine love
which it undergoes will include the absolute sovereignty and
transcendent power of the God to whom it belongs, because it
is in fact his very Spirit. So far from being merely a subjective
velleity, love has an energy and a force of its own, like a
"torrent of the Spirit of God", whose power and initiative can
actually be experienced by the soul

> with such force that it seems to her that all the rivers of the
> world are coming upon her and assailing her, and she feels
> that all her previous actions and passions are overwhelmed
> by it.
>
> (*Cant.* 14:9)

For all its intimacy, the love ofGod is unutterably awesome. If
it casts out the fear of punishment, it leaves even greater place
for the religious 'fear' of the divine *tremendum*. This seems to
be John's most common term for love's work, that it "assails"
(*embiste*) the soul,[20] and sometimes with such a relentless
purpose that it can be fearfully oppressive (*esquiva*), pursuing
its purifying designs so unremittingly that it truly seems to the
soul "that God has become cruel to her and bitter" (*L.F.* 1:20).
And even though the presence is recognized as that of the
Beloved, the suddenness and power of his visitation can cause

[20] *L.F.* 1:19, 22, 25, 35; 2:9, 3. *Cant.* 13:3f.

the soul a great terror (*el gran pavor*) so that she will beg him to withdraw his loving gaze upon her (*Cant.* 13:3).

However, such strength belongs not just to the divine love coming from God upon the soul, as though the latter's passivity under it should be all the more frail and helpless. How could God's love, which is the source of his overflowing creativity, diminish what he has thus made? Therefore, to undergo that love is to be taken possession of by it[21] and thus to share in its "awesome strength" (*terrible fortaleza*):

> 'Her neck reclining on the gentle arms of the Beloved' . . . is for the soul to have its strength now united—or rather its weakness—in the strength of God; . . . wherein our weakness, reclining upon him and transformed in him, has now the strength of God himself.
>
> (*Cant.* 22:7)

Thus we return again to that constant theme of St. John's spirituality: by being true, through free consent, to his necessary ontological passivity under God, a person enters into the full possession of his own powers. For like everything else, these are held only as a gift from God, and their truly effective exercise can be realized only by a constant docility which allows them to be subsumed into His power.

For this reason, the strength of love is closely associated with its intrinsic singleness or concentration, and its power to unify and integrate. We have already seen how that "one single hair" of love threads all the other virtues together, informing them with vigour and power.[22] But it would be a mistake to ascribe this unifying function of love solely to God's sovereign will, as though imposed upon the soul and doing violence to its natural complexity. There is also a foundation in human nature for love's complete penetration of the soul: for it belongs to man's will, the sanctuary of his freedom and responsibility, to guide the other powers and so to inform them with moral and personal value:

---

[21]*Cant.* 14:9; 20:1; 9:4; 12:7; *L.F.* 1:1; 3:79.
[22]*Cant.* 24:7; 28:8; 30:9; 31:3ff.

> the strength of the soul consists in its faculties, passions and
> desires, all of which are governed by the will.
>
> (*Asc.* III, 16, 2)

The cruel irony of undisciplined desires is that, in spite of their
natural vitality, their ultimate effect is to disperse the soul's
strength and to make it weak and flaccid; but insofar as the
will is possessed by the love of God, it can dedicate all these
powers to him also, "recollected in one single desire for God"
(*Asc.* I, 10, 1). Purity of love, then, is not a lack of richness,
but an intense concentration. This is the "brevity" of prayer
which penetrates the heavens (*L.F.* 1:33). It is the divinely
bestowed harmony celebrated in the Song of Solomon: "The
King made me enter the cellar of wine and set in order charity
in me" (Sol 2:4), out of which acts of love.

> are as much more delectable and meritorious than those
> made by the soul, as the mover and infuser of this love—
> namely God—is better than the soul.
>
> (*L.F.* 3:50)

Even "more meritorious"! Because it derives from God's
incomparable strength, that love will be so much more effective
than if it should arise merely out of finite human resources, yet
at the same time the human person is glorified in it because he
has freely committed his own responsibility and his willingness
into that movement of love.

'PASSION'

Without meaning to diminish love's perfection and strength,
we must recognize the essential role that suffering has to play
in St. John's conception of charity. To be passive under the
work of love, to undergo or to 'suffer' it, will also include
suffering in its stricter sense of pain and diminishment. As we
have seen, love is not only the goal of the spiritual life but is
also essential to the process of transformation:

> For it must be known that the same fire of love which
> afterwards is united with the soul and glorifies it is that
> which previously assailed it in order to purge it.
>
> (*L.F.* 1:19; c.f. also *D.N.* II, 10, 1f)

This is a further great security against John's spirituality of love being debased into sentimentality. Love's own essential purpose is a "union of likeness" (*Asc.* II, 5, 3). But if the soul is unlike God not only in its natural contingency, but also in its distorting marks of sin, then the immediate task of love can only be to rectify the disorder. Love simply requires the truth (*Cant.* 13:12). Therefore, all that is said of the extreme suffering of the night of spirit might as well be attributed to love as to faith; it is a "purifying *and loving* knowledge or divine light" which is penetrating the soul (*D.N.* II, 10, 1), inexorably bringing to light the roots of sin which vitiate perfect union. John will not allow love to be counterfeited by compromise with sin. He knows that God's utterly merciful love does far better—it renews us by destroying sin. Indeed, just as the fire of love reaches to the most deeply rooted imperfections, that is, when the soul's suffering is most intimate and intense, it is then that love "acts with even more force and vehemence in preparing its most inward part to possess it" (*D.N.* II, 10, 7). Since it seems that "the very substance" of the soul is being consumed in this purification, then the faculty of loving must share in the agony no less than any other. Jeremiah laments, "In the night my mouth is pierced with sorrows" (Lam 30:17); by which St. John understands him to mean "the will, which is transpierced with these pains that tear the soul to pieces" (*D.N.* II, 9, 8).

Once again a cautionary note is necessary here. In the *Dark Night*, John expounds the sufferings of love at such length and with such fervent intensity that one might be inclined to understand them—suffering and love—as too simply identical. Intensity of inner experience can reinforce deviation as well as growth, and could topple into introverted, morbid fascination with suffering. Therefore it is essential to remember that this experience of radical purification is placed in its true context in the *Living Flame*, where it is but one element in a movement

towards blessed union (*L.F.* 1:18-26). The real nature of love
transcends any partial human perception of it in this life,
whether as delight or as pain.

Quite apart, therefore, from the mortal conflict of holiness
opposed to sin, there is a kind of suffering which arises simply
from the absolute transcendence of God over his finite creature:

> the affection of love which is to be given to [the soul] in the
> divine union of love is divine, . . . transcending every affec-
> tion and feeling of the will and every one of its desires.
>
> (*D.N.* II, 9, 3)

That is, it surpasses every particular desire. But there is a
certain ground of desire which is coextensive with the soul's
very being, made in the image of God—the natural capacity of
its "deep caverns":

> that which they are capable of containing, which is God, is
> deep and infinite; and thus in a certain sense their capacity
> will be infinite, and likewise their thirst will be infinite,
>
> (*L.F.* 3:22)

The deep reaches of these caverns are revealed by the light of
grace. The more a soul is purified by the fire of love, the
clearer will be its spiritual vision of all things, including itself.
It becomes aware of its own unsearchable capacity, knowing
experientially how totally it is made for union with God, but
also how completely that fulfillment lies beyond its own
resources. This is not a speculative philosophical insight. It is
the experience of radical "emptiness" by which love prepares
the will, straining its capacity to ever greater limits in anticipation of an ever greater fruition.[23] It takes the form of
consuming desire:

> Of this manner, then, are the yearnings of love of which this
> soul becomes conscious when it made some progress in this
> spiritual purgation. For it rises up by night (that is, in this

---

[23]C.f. above, chap 4, *Asc.* II, 6, 4; *D.N.* II, 21, 11; *Cant.* 6; *L.F.* 3:18-22.

purifying darkness) according to the affections of the will.... For, being in darkness, it feels itself to be without God and to be dying of love for him. And this is that impatient love wherein the soul cannot long subsist without receiving or dying. Such was Rachel's desire for children when she said to Jacob: 'Give me children, or I shall die'.

(*D.N.* II, 13, 8; Gen 30:1)

Perhaps it is not too contrived to see a particularly loaded meaning in the reference to such vehement desire as "impatient love" (*amor impaciente*). It refuses to rest quietly, it is a "passivity" which is urgently turned to receive.

The spirit feels itself here to be deeply and passionately in love, for this spiritual enkindling produces the passion of love. And, inasmuch as this love is infused, it is passive rather than active, and thus it begets in the soul a strong passion of love.

(*D.N.* II, 11, 2)

Passivity here reaches a most intense and complex meaning in the spiritual life. There is first the simple ontological fact of being changed by a divine power of love. Moreover, that love of God is not just concealed as a metaphysical substratum under the natural activity of the soul; in this mystical grace the soul is conscious of *being moved* to love, not only by the goodness and beauty of God as the intended object, but also 'subjectively', by a powerful source lying even deeper than its own personal resources. That supernatural movement from within catches up the emotions or passions, thus marking the whole experience as at once vividly spiritual and palpably sensuous:

this passive love does not now directly strike the will, for the will is free and this enkindling of love is a passion of love rather than a free act of the will; for this heat of love strikes the substance of the soul and thus moves the affections passively.

(*D.N.* II, 13, 3)

What John indicates here by "the substance of the soul", is that even the experienced source of the movement is anterior to the soul's own deliberate willingness. Nevertheless, human freedom is not uninvolved, as though the whole experience were simply an inspired but superficial emotion; the moral reaches of the human spirit are also caught up in the divinely infused stream of passion, John even using the bold language that "the will is taken captive and loses its liberty, according as the impetus and power of its passion carry it away" (*Ibid.*). In a strict sense, of course, the will is by definition free and cannot lose its liberty. John here declares that there is a free commitment by the soul of its deepest power of loving—"what the soul does here is to give its consent" (*D.N.* II, 11, 2): but that it is a *consequent* commitment into a stream of loving whose initiative and power lie clearly prior to and beyond its own deliberation—

> actions of God rather than of the soul . . . ; the warmth and strength and temper and passion of love belong only to the love of God which enters increasingly into union with [the soul].
>
> (*D.N.* II, 11, 2)

This extraordinary pre-emption from within by God's love, "for which reason it is called a passion of love rather than a free act of the will" (II, 13, 3), is therefore not an abdication by the soul of personal responsibility, nor God's suspension of human freedom. It is a self-dedication into the origin and goal of all human resources, God's sustaining love.

DEATH

We have already met several allusions to a death of love. These are not just for the sake of rhetorical intensity, as if to indicate poetically the extremity of suffering involved in preparation for union. They bear a literal meaning: for in fact death is one essential moment in the mystery of transformation into new life, which is identical with love and which stands at the centre of the spiritual life. As a preliminary observation, we should note that for St. John, following the New Testament, the meaning of death and new life is two-fold. It can mean simply the end of this mortal life, with an implication of breaking through into the life of the vision of God.[24] More often it refers to the dying into a new 'theological life' of grace, the death to sin for a holy life in God:

> that which the soul here calls death is all that is meant by the 'old man',
>
> (*L.F.* 2:33; c.f. Eph 4:22-24)

that is, the selfish immersion of one's life in merely contingent concerns. And, as St. Paul exhorts, "we must put off the old man ... and put on the new man who, in the likeness of the omnipotent God is created in justice and holiness" (*Ibid.*). But most significantly, apart from a few occasions in which John wishes to emphasize the difference between beatific vision and the life of faith, these two meanings, of physical and of theological dying, tend to coalesce:

> it must be known that the soul lives where it loves rather than in the body which it animates, because it has not its life in the body, but rather gives it to the body, and lives through love in [God whom] it loves.
>
> (*Cant.* 8:3)

The mystery of death indicates that the spiritual life certainly is not just a matter of some subtle techniques, nor even of some deeper attitudes which are adopted as fitting ornaments to one's fundamental, self-possessed existence. The love of God is deadly serious, undoing and reshaping the very substance of a person's life:

---

[24]*Cant.* 8; 11; *L.F.* 1:29f; 2:32.

the soul finds itself burning in the fire and flame of love, so
much so that it appears to be consumed in the flame which
causes it to go forth from itself and be wholly renewed and
enter upon another mode of being; like the phoenix, that is,
burned up and reborn anew.

(Cant. 1:17)

And so, the physical death of a human is not merely biological,
as though it were simply an accidental circumstance of one's
'real' life of grace. The end of this mortal life, because it touches
the whole of one's being, is in itself a profoundly personal and
theological reality, all the more so inasmuch as the soul has
come into a more complete possession of its true life in the
love of God:

> with regard to the natural dying of souls that reach [trans-
> forming union], though the manner of their death from the
> natural standpoint is similar to that of others, yet in the
> cause and mode of their death there is a great difference.
> For while the deaths of others may be caused by infirmities
> or length of days, when these souls die, although it may be
> from some infirmity or from old age, their spirits are wrested
> away by nothing less than some loving impulse and en-
> counter far loftier and of greater power and strength than
> any in the past, for it has succeeded in breaking the web and
> bearing away a jewel, which is the spirit.
>
> *(L.F.* 1:30)

John here exemplifies that zestful other-worldliness of Spanish
mysticism which can so scandalize our circumspect and secular
age. However, no charge of escapism can be sustained against
him. The very drive towards new life through death is fuelled
by his intense experiences of love in this life. While this account
from *The Living Flame* is of a very rare and perfect consummation, the death of a saint, it is still related to all other
experiences of the love of God as their perfect exemplar.
Therefore, just as a last supreme ecstasy achieves the liberation
of the spirit into a new and glorious mode of existence, so

every spark of charity is an impulse which, whether recognized as such or not, heads toward that critical culmination in death. Through its infused orientation towards fulfilment in God, the whole of human life is penetrated by the reality of dying. Bearing this inner strain towards perfection of love not yet attained, St. John feels this mortal life more and more to be a deprivation of true life:

> natural life is to [the soul] as death, since through it she is deprived of the spiritual life wherein she has all her being and life through nature, and all her operations and affections through love.
>
> (*Cant.* 8:3)

Taken merely in itself, "to desire to die is an imperfection of nature" (*Cant.* 11:8); and although John does not speculate on the mysterious origin of death in sin, the mere fact of death is recognized clearly as conflict and disharmony, the sign of radical lack of integrity (*Cant.* 8:3). But animated by the love of God, that desire heads through this negative moment into its ultimate meaning, "that what is mortal may be swallowed up by life" (2 Cor 5:4; *Cant.* 11:9), "death is swallowed up in victory" (1 Cor 15:54; Is 25:8; *L.F.* 2:34).

Such dying through love is obviously the very antithesis of bleak despair or desperate defiance. And this is so, not merely because of the positive end of new life which lies beyond death: the actual event of death can itself be a profound affirmation. In one respect, of course, it is the greatest of all the passivities a human can undergo. Its inevitability and universality make it the great leveller, coming upon the frail creature as a sovereign overriding demand and manifesting in a most severe way the individual's total subjection to the common law of mortality. However, John explores even this universal passivity to death in an unusual and surprising way—a further sign of the great 'reversal' already achieved by God's grace. For he does not argue that death's inexorable coming tramples over natural reluctance and fear, but, on the contrary, that its advent will not be commanded even by the most fervent desires and entreaties: "Let the vision of Thee and Thy beauty slay me" (*Cant.* 11), "Break the web of this sweet encounter" (*L. F.* 1:29). And so there is something awesomely 'other' about the mystery of death. If our life is so radically given, just so is it radically taken.

On the other hand, that event of spoliation which comes upon the soul can be a fulfilment of its deepest desire. The "passion of love", in which the deepest reaches of man's willingness are caught up into the antecedent impulse of the love of God, here finds its perfection. The spiritual life is an ever more perfect personal assent to being possessed by God, which John again captures beautifully in a delicate inter-penetration of action and passivity:

> 'Wandering love-stricken, I lost my way and was found' . . . that is, she allowed herself to be lost of set purpose (*dejarse perder de industria*).
>
> (*Cant.* 29:10)

Complete submission to the law of mortality as an imperative loving call from God forms a unity with the active consum-mation of self from within. To lose one's life thus is to achieve perfect self-possession (*Cant.* 29:11), a personal achievement through all the resources of one's spiritual being, but at the same time a 'being found' by God's creative and gratuitous love.

CHRIST

Christ is the key to all of this. The mystery of the soul's death and new life is a form of divine love because it is a participation in the paschal mystery of Christ:

> Christ is the Way, and this Way is death to our natural selves in things both of sense and of spirit; . . . we are to die following the example of Christ, for he is our example and light.
>
> (*Asc.* II, 7, 9)

The call to the soul to lose her life is authentic only inasmuch as it comes from the Beloved Lord of the Gospels—"for my sake"; and St. John of the Cross accepts St. Paul's "to die is gain" only because it proceeds from the realization that "to live is Christ" (Phil 1:21; *Cant.* 29:10). It is essential to the saint's doctrine of the Cross that it is wholly an echo of the summons of Christ: no human ingenuity, no matter how spiritual and sublime, could be adequate to the goal of divine life. Just as Jesus' utter desolation was undergone in pure obedience to his Father's will, so the soul's actual following of that Way must not be undertaken presumptuously, as of right, but only as a loving acceptance of the Lord's gratuitous invitation,

> giving oneself up to suffering for Christ's sake, and to total annihilation.
>
> (*Asc.* II, 7, 8)

The divine transcending power of love—"for God's sake"[25]—is manifested completely in the features of the Incarnate Word through whom the mystery is revealed—"for Christ's sake". There is an arresting contrast in the biographical traditions concerning St. Thomas Aquinas and St. John of the Cross. In reply to the Lord's offer of reward for his services, Thomas reveals a splendid loving devotion to the Giver himself of all blessings, beyond any particular gift: '*Nihil nisi te, Domine*', "Nothing but yourself, O Lord". That would seem to be the perfect model of John's doctrine of genuine loving faith which reaches unconditionally towards God alone beyond any partial fulfilment. In a similar colloquy, however, John's answer might seem to be less consistent with his doctrine of absolute transcendence, and more attached to a particular way of devotion to the Cross: '*Senor, lo que quiero me deis es trabajos que padecer por vos y que sea yo menospreciado y tenido en poco*': "Lord, what I want you to give me is tribulation to

---

[25]"For to love is to work to despoil and strip oneself for God's sake of all that is not God" (*Asc.* II, 5, 7).

suffer for your sake, and that I might be despised and held of little account". However, we must recognize here the full import of "for your sake". The choice for suffering is for a "sacramental"—that is, a mysterious but utterly real—sharing in the being of Christ. Not for a "parallel" form of existence (impossible presumption!), but for Christ's very own:

> Let Christ crucified be sufficient for thee, and with him suffer and rest.
>
> (*Points*, 13)

By his obedient embracing of the mission given by his Father, Jesus has become the personification of that mission, he himself is the Way. Therefore, the things he does and suffers are embraced by his friends only because those things belong to him and indeed mediate him through the communion of love:

> loving his bitter trials and his death because of their great love for him.
>
> (*Asc.* II, 7, 12)

In Christ himself, the Incarnate Word, 'bodily', and not just in his discursive doctrine, are hidden all the treasures of wisdom and knowledge of God (*Asc.* II, 22, 6; Col 2:3, 9).

At this point we might pause to resume very simply how the logic of the Gospel is thus fulfilled in John's experience and teaching. The reality of the spiritual ascent, its every step and its goal, is love, and the goal of human existence is nothing but God himself. But God is love, and Christ is divine love incarnate, God's gift of himself to the world. And so, for all his apophatic power, St. John of the Cross bears witness to a mystical world—the world of the gospel—which is diametrically opposed to a mysticism which would refine away the concrete and the personal in favour of immersion in a nameless One.

WISDOM

The divine love realized in Christ also determines the nature of contemplative Wisdom. In some respect it is true that one must first perceive the beautiful in order to love it. Nevertheless, the deepest kind of understanding is not so much a prelude to love as its fruit. "The heart has its reasons which reason does not know" (Pascal), and for St. John of the Cross, true love, far from being blind and voluntaristic, gives rise to a whole new dimension of knowing: the "secret wisdom" of mystical insight "is communicated and infused into the soul through love" (*D.N.* II, 17, 2). Moreover, the length and breadth and height and depth of God's own Wisdom is revealed to be love in Christ's sacrificial death—which therefore remains the central fount of the mystic's understanding:

> the soul that truly desires divine wisdom first desires suffering so that it might enter it—yes, into the thicket of the Cross.
>
> (*Cant.* 36:13; Eph 3:18)

The desire to share in the mystery of the Cross is therefore more than a sentiment of solidarity with the Beloved: it is an instinct for the truth. Since in Christ crucified the utter dereliction of sin, from which we would avert our eyes, is made manifest, then this tree of knowledge of good and evil is the only way into the joy of knowing God's love as it really is— redeeming, merciful love. "He that seeks not the Cross of Christ seeks not the glory of Christ" (*Sayings*, 100). In his abandonment and death, Christ exposes to judgement sin's refusal of love: but at that very moment he buries that refusal in his loving submission to the worst it can do. The "moment of his death, when he was annihilated in his soul", is the focus of his whole life's mission—"the reconciliation and union of mankind, through grace, with God" (*Asc.* II, 7, 11). This is the reason why St. John insists that the contemplative must not avert his eyes from the Cross. Only there is love's exigence for truth fulfilled, in such a way that the Cross is transfigured from being a sign of condemnation into God's perfect "word of consolation" in every need:

> gaze upon my Son, who is subject to me and bound by love of me, and afflicted, and you will see how fully he answers you.
>
> (*Asc.* II, 22, 6)

By that "gaze" the soul enters into the Wisdom of God, which probes the heart in order to heal it. Just as the Cross is transformed by God's love from being a sign of condemnation to that of mercy, so the disfiguring marks of sin are not simply erased, but are transfigured into marks of redeeming love. That is true primarily of the wounds of Jesus, the sinless one whom God "made to be sin" (2 Cor 5:21): at his resurrection, appearing to the disciples to manifest the new life triumphant in himself, "he showed them his hands and his side" (Jn 20:20), wounds now standing not against them in judgement, but for them in loving mercy. Just so in the disciple himself: there is nothing which has gone into the making of his existence, even those experiences which included a refusal of God, which falls outside the ambit of grace. The receiving of God's mercy transforms the disfigurements of sin into marks of love:

> And this burn of love has the property that, when it touches a soul, whether this soul be wounded by other wounds such as miseries and sins, or whether it be whole, it at once leaves it wounded with love. Thus wounds due to another cause have become wounds of love.
>
> (*L.F.* 2:7)

This image is most readily understood in terms of the forgiveness of one's own sin—the wonder, the abounding joy in recognizing in Jesus an unconditional love, "to the end" (Jn 13:1), an effective reconciling love regardless of how disastrously one might have refused him. So we can hear in this sentence the inner experience which St. John had of himself—

as *the* sinner, redeemed—just as Paul had before him (1 Tim 1:15), and every one of the saints. But John affirms that it is also true of our *miserias*, of all our experiences of limitation, inadequacy, failure—physical, temperamental, intellectual. In even these features of mundane existence which one experiences as so inescapably poor, sometimes so trivial, and, to unsympathetic human eyes, so sheerly unlovely—in these, too, one is loved, and thus they may be changed from marks of self-dislike to the blessed joy of the poor. The physical horror of the wounds of the sickness that killed him—no chance of idealizing away the raw ugliness of them when they stamp the flesh—became signs for him of a communion with the tender mercy of God in the Passion of Christ. And finally, we must include the marks he bore of the failings and sins of others. Dragged out of a dark prison cell in Toledo to be humiliated and beaten by his brethren, he returned to the cell to write a Canticle celebrating the love of God, a love which could infuse into his heart such a true loving forgiveness that even those wretched events of human cruelty served to carry a redeeming meaning. "Where there is no love, put love and you will draw love out" (Letter XXII). This is the "foolishness of God", the secret wisdom of His loving mercy, which love itself impells Him to reveal even to His creatures:

> for true and perfect love can keep nothing hidden from the person loved.
>
> (*Cant.* 23:)

HOLY SPIRIT

Christ, then, is the Word revealing God as love. It is by the gift of His Holy Spirit that one hears that Word, and the Spirit is itself the reality of that revealed love living in the soul.

> In this breathing of the Holy Spirit through the soul, which is his visitation to her in love, the Spouse who is the Son of God communicates himself to her after a lofty manner. For this purpose he first sends his Spirit, who is his forerunner,

as he did to the Apostles, to prepare for him the dwelling of
the soul his Bride.

(Cant. 17:8)

Thus, the Spirit is at the same time God's present gift of
himself to the soul, and also the preparation for an even more
complete union with Christ who sends him. This is the Holy
Spirit leading the soul into all truth through an integral hearing
of God's Word of love (*Asc.* II, 29, 1; 29, 6).

INTO TRINITY

The hearing of God's Word through the gift of his love is
therefore an essentially Trinitarian grace, and it is this divine
relationship which constitutes the new life into which the soul
enters through Christ's death of love:

> For God said that the Father and the Son and the Holy
> Spirit would come to him that loved him, and make their
> abode in him, and this would come to pass by his making
> him love and dwell in the Father and the Son and the Holy
> Spirit, in the life of God.
>
> *(L.F.* Prol, 2)

To speak of the life of God is certainly to mean something
'objective'—in one respect it must always remain the wholly
Other, the transcendent goal of the creature's religious dynamism—but that life is a fullness of spiritual being which is
therefore completely realized in personal understanding and
love. There is not any more fundamental, non-personal divine
foundation. Thus, the gift of love in the Holy Spirit can only
mean that man shares in that inner life of the Trinity:

> [the soul] may breathe in God the same breath of love that
> the Father breathes in the Son and the Son in the Father,

> which is the same Holy Spirit that God breathes into the
> soul in the Father and the Son.
>
> (*Cant.* 39:3)

Such a sharing in divine life means that the soul's existence
becomes wholly subsumed into loving knowledge, not merely
by observing it from outside, but as participating in the
relationship of the Son to the Father, for "God has sent the
Spirit of his Son into your hearts, crying to the Father" (*Cant.*
39:4; c.f. Gal 4:6). This is the essence of St. John's contemplation—to manifest ever more deeply in the soul the relationship of the Son to the Father in the Holy Spirit which is
implicit in faith, in such a way that contemplation itself
becomes an inner function of that relationship. It will become
less an accidental 'practice', and, analogously with God, more
the full expression of her life as love:

> the Holy Spirit proceeds from the contemplation and
> wisdom of the Father and the Son, and is breathed—so
> here the Spouse calls this love of the soul air, because it
> proceeds from the contemplation and knowledge which at
> this time the soul has of God ... even as love is union of
> the Father and the Son, even so also is it union of the soul
> with God.
>
> (*Cant.* 13:11)

As we have already remarked, divine being is wholly personal;
for this reason St. John insists that this mystical perfection of
loving wisdom does not lie as a perfection beyond the sphere
of baptismal grace, but is its proper realization:

> For, since God grants the soul the favour of uniting her in
> the most Holy Trinity, wherein she becomes deiform and
> God by participation, how is it a thing incredible that she
> should also perform her work of understanding, knowledge
> and love—or to express it better, should have it performed
> in the Trinity, together with it, like the Trinity Itself.
>
> (*Cant.* 39:4)

Indeed, not only is it the proper flowering of the new life of grace, but also the perfection of the soul's own natural being, "for it was to this end that he created her in his image and likeness" (*Ibid.*).

GIFT OF BEING

' . . .should have it performed . . . (*la tenga obrada en la Trinidad*)': it should be clear from all we have been saying of this divine life of love that it is indeed primarily God's own life and that therefore there must be a most radical passivity on the part of the soul drawn into it:

> in this flame the acts of the will are united and rise upward, being carried away and absorbed in the flame of the Holy Spirit.
>
> (*L.F.* 1:4)

To speak of 'absorption' is strong language indeed, conjuring as it does echoes of the perennial mystical temptation to a pantheism or a monism in which passivity becomes absolute, a supposed annihilation of all individuality in the creature. And yet, even when St. John likewise asserts that in transforming union "the soul can perform no acts, but it is the Holy Spirit that performs them" (*Ibid.*), we can surely understand this, as we have done the "passion of love", not as a suppression of the soul's being and action, but as a divine transcendental embracing so as to confirm them. The personal is here supreme, not an undifferentiated, nameless Absolute. Love is now seen to touch not only the apex of man's freedom and individuality ("in its deepest centre . . . it gives its will and consent", *L.F.* 1:9), but also to involve God in the intimate determinations of his three-Personal being:

> O sweet burn! O delectable wound!
> O soft hand! O delicate touch!

The soul explains how the three Persons of the Most Holy

Trinity, Father, Son and Holy Spirit, are they that effect within it this divine work of union.

(L.F. 2:1)

The stream of love into which the soul is caught up does not flow forth from God as if leaving him sublimely uninvolved, but is itself God's love personified.

There now emerges the astounding active corollary to the soul's passivity. By the grace of transforming union, the soul becomes so perfectly receptive—"its only concern is now the receiving of God" (*L.F.* 1:9)—that the deep caverns of its spiritual powers become completely infused with the life of God, wholly translucent to his glory (*L.F.* 3:77). By a certain "overflowing" they become a new place for God's own loving wisdom (*Cant.* 37:8). And so, within the truth of God's unassailable transcendence, and deriving from his absolute initiative, there is realized also a certain "equality" (*igualdad*) between him and his creature, now made his friend and his son, which is essential to true love.[26] The gift of grace has raised a creature into a hitherto unimaginable relationship of "reciprocal love" (*L.F.* 3:78), for he acts now not merely out of his own finite resources, "giving his will and consent" (*L.F.* 1:9), but that very action as belonging to the soul is informed with divine power:

> the Holy Spirit moves the soul to perform them; wherefore all its acts are divine, since it is moved and impelled to them by God.

(L.F. 1:4 et passim)

This emergence of true action from passivity, of life from death, of fulness from dispossession, is not really a 'paradox' at all; it is the natural 'logic' of love.

In the consummation of love, the Spirit wholly informs and brings to perfection action and passivity. Perhaps the most

---

[26]*Asc.* I, 5, 1; *L.F.* 3:6; *Cant.* 22:7; 24:5; 28:1; 32:6.

integral form of action born from passivity, is that of *giving* which arises out of *receiving*. That mystery therefore runs as a leitmotiv through Jesus' 'priestly' prayer to his Father before his Passion (Jn 17), and St. John of the Cross adopts it as the truest form constituting the union of love:

> all mine are thine, and thine are mine.... The glory which thou hast given me I have given to them, that they may be one even as we are one .... Father, I desire that they also, whom thou hast given me, may be with me where I am, to behold my glory which thou hast given me ... that the love with which thou hast loved me may be in them and I in them.
>
> (Jn 17; *Cant.* 36:5; 39:5; *L.F.* 3:79; 3:82)

The inner form of love is revealed archetypally in the Triune God who is love: the Father giving himself wholly in speaking his Word, begetting his Son;[27] the Son wholly given back in loving obedience to his Father;[28] and that self-giving of both personified in the Holy Spirit, which is also the full self-giving of God to man.[29] The soul possessed by that Spirit is taken up into the same divine pattern of complete self-giving:

> Even as God is giving Himself to the soul with free and gracious will, even so likewise the soul, having a will that is freer and more generous in proportion as it has a greater degree of union with God, is giving God in God to Himself, and thus the gift of the soul to God is true and entire.
>
> (*L.F.* 3:78)

The gift of God's love perfectly received so enriches the soul that it is able to give back more than its own poor contingent self:

[27] *Asc.* II, 22, 5f; *Cant.* 36:5; 39:3f.
[28] *Asc.* II, 7, 11; *Cant.* 36:5.
[29] *Cant.* 39:3f; *L.F.* 3:82.

> And herein the soul pays God all that it owes him; inasmuch
> as of its own will it gives as much as it has received of him
> . . . it is giving to God that which is his own and which is
> appropriate to him according to his infinite Being. . . . And
> this he takes with gratitude, as something belonging to the
> soul that it gives to him, and in that same gift he also loves
> the soul anew.
>
> (*L.F.* 3:78f)

Mutual giving and receiving in gratitude is a "eucharistic"
love, and whilst its essence is to be wholly given away, aban-
doning all possession in favour of the Beloved, the effect of
this 'new wine' is an upward spiral of love and eschatological
joy:

> from all these wonders and grandeurs of God which are
> infused into the soul there overflows for her one fruition
> and one delight of love alone, which is the drink of the Holy
> Spirit, which she offers at once to her God, the Word-
> Spouse, with great tenderness of love. . . . For as God tastes
> it, he gives it to her to taste, and as she tastes it, she gives it
> back to him to taste, so that they both taste of it together.
>
> (*Cant.* 27:8)

The perfection of the spiritual life in the dawn light of
mystical union and the bright day of beatific vision thus
resumes in itself all that has been of value in the growth
through the dark night. Sharing the intimate life of the Trinity,
St. John attains the full realization of his original being and
potentiality as the image of God, and that of course includes
the complete actuation of all his personal spiritual resources of
knowledge and love. Liberated from the bonds of sin, he
enjoys a perfect integration and self-possession which enables
him to achieve the greatest of all possible works: to "lose his
life" by the free gift of himself in love to God who is his life
and joy. He enters into a fulness of life, experiencing all things
in their truth, and preserving an unrestricted liberty of spirit in
them all. And yet all of this is an absolutely gratuitous gift.

Even the self-giving is a grace, deriving from God's first gift of himself. And so he lives his new life of love only because he receives it, only because he undergoes (*padecer*) his own creation and re-creation in God's image by God's transcendent power. Like every saint, John of the Cross manifests in his life and his spiritual power an always wider and deeper truth: all his glory is from within, from God in his deepest centre.

Appendix

Chronological Outline of the Life of St. John of the Cross

1542   Juan de Yepes born at Fontiveros (Avila), youngest of three sons in a family of poor weavers. His father, Gonzalo, had been disinherited for offending against the *honra* of his hidalgo family by marrying Catalina Alvarez for love and "below his station".

c. 1544   Death of Gonzalo de Yepes. Catalina subsequently takes her young family to Arévalo, then to Medina del Campo.

1556-62   Lives and works in a hospital in Medina. Elements of secondary education at College of Society of Jesus.

1563   Receives the Carmelite habit under the name of Juan de San Matías, entering the novitiate at St. Anne's, Medina.

1564   After profession of vows, to the University of Salamanca for the three-year course in Arts (1564-7).

1567   Ordained priest. Intends to transfer to the Carthusian Order; meets St. Teresa (then aged 52), who persuades him to join her Discalced Reform. Begins a year's course in theology at Salamanca.

1568   November 28: takes the vows of the Reform as Juan de la Cruz at Duruelo with two other friars in the first foundation of the Discalced. For the next few years involved in some new foundations and the spiritual formation of the Reform.

1571	Rector of the College at Alacalà de Henares.

| 1572 | To Avila as confessor to the Convent of the Incarnation where Teresa is Prioress. Remains until 1577. |

| 1577 | December: kidnapped by those opposed to the Reform and imprisoned in the Priory at Toledo. While in prison composes several poems including much of the 'Spiritual Canticle' and perhaps 'Dark Night'. |

| 1578 | August: escapes from prison. Appointed as Vicar of Discalced foundation of El Calvario in Andalusia. Confessor to Carmelite nuns at Beàs. Begins commentaries *Ascent of Mount Carmel* and *Spiritual Canticle*. |

| 1579 | June: founds College at Baeza; serves as Prior here until 1582. |

| 1580 | Death of his mother, Catalina. |

| 1581 | November: last meeting with St. Teresa, at Avila. |

| 1582 | Prior of Los Mártires at Granada (until 1588). During this time completes prose treatises. |

| 1585 | *Living Flame of Love*, written in fifteen days. Appointed Vicar-Provincial of Andalusia; makes several foundations in next couple of years. |

| 1588 | June: attends first General Chapter of Discalced in Madrid; elected First Definitor. August: Prior of Segovia. |

1591

June: after scurrilous campaign of calumny against him, and growing tension with Vicar-General Nicholas Doria overdirection of Reform, deprived of offices; decision to send him to Mexico (later revoked), sent out of the way to La Penuela. September: falls ill with fever; travels to Ubeda. December 14: dies in the monastery at Ubeda.

1675

January 25: beatified by Clement X.

1726

December 26: canonized by Benedict XIII.

1926

August 24: declared Doctor of the Church by Pius XI.

Select Bibliography

Texts.

San Juan de la Cruz, *Obras Completas*, 2ª edicion, Madrid: Editorial de Espiritualidad, 1980.

Vida y Obras Completas de San Juan de la Cruz, 4ª edicion, Madrid: Biblioteca de Autores Cristianos, 1960.

The Complete Works of St. John of the Cross, Doctor of the Church, trans. and ed. E. Allison Peers, Wheathampstead, Hertfordshire, 1974.

The Complete Works of St. John of the Cross, trans. Kieran Kavanaugh, OCD and Otilio Rodriguez, OCD, Washington, I.C.S. Publications, 1979.

The Poems of St. John of the Cross, the Spanish text with a translation by Roy Campbell, London: The Harvill Press, 1951.

Biographies.

Fr. Bruno, ODC, *St. John of the Cross*, London: Sheed & Ward, 1936.

Crisogono de Jesus, OCD, *The Life of St. John of the Cross*, London: Longmans, 1958.

Studies.

Balthasar, Hans Urs von, "St. John of the Cross", *The Glory of the Lord*, volume III: Studies in Theological Styles: Lay Styles, Edinburgh: T. & T. Clark, 1986, pp 105-171.

Baruzi, J., *Saint Jean de la Croix et le problème de l'expérience mystique*, 2de ed., Paris, 1931.

A Benedictine of Stanbrook, *Mediaeval Mystical Tradition and St. John of the Cross*, London: Burns & Dates, 1954.

Bord, André, *Memoire et espérance chez Jean de la Croix*, Paris, 1971.

Bouillard, H., 'Mystique, metaphysique et foi chretienne', *RSR*, 51, 1963, pp 30-82. 'La sagesse mystique selon Saint Jean de la Croix', *RSR*, 50, 1962, pp 481-529.

Crisógono de Jesus Sacramentado OCD, *San Jan de la Cruz, su obra cientifica y su obra literaria*, Avila, 1929.

Cummins, Norbert, OCD, An Introduction to St. John of the Cross, Darlington Carmel, 1986.

Efren de la Madre de Dios, OCD, *San Jaun de la Cruz y el Misterio de la Santisima Trinidad en la vida espiritual*, Zaragoza, 1947.

Foresti, Fabrizio OCD, *Sinai and Carmel; the Biblical Roots of the Doctrine of St. John of the Cross*, Darlington Carmel, 1981.

Florisoone, Michel, *Esthétique et Mystique d'après Sainte Thérèse d'Avila et Saint Jean de la Croix*, Paris, 1956.

Francois de Sainte Marie, OCD, *Initiation à Saint Jean de la Croix*, Paris, 1946.

Gabriel de Sainte Marie-Madeleine, OCD, 'Le Cantique de l'amour', *Sanjuanistica*, Rome, 1943, pp 87-132.

Gabriel de Sainte Marie-Madeleine, OCD, 'Le problème de la contemplation unitive', *Eph C*, 1, 1947, pp 5-53, 245-277.

——————, *Saint John of the Cross, Doctor of Divine Love and Contemplation*, Cork: Mercier Press, 1947.

Lucien-Marie de Saint Joseph, OCD, *L'expérience de Dieu. Actualité du message de Saint Jean de la Croix*, Paris, 1968.

——————, 'Expérience mystique et expression symbolique chez saint Jean de la Croix', *Et C*, 39, 1960, pp 29-51.

Fr. Marie-Eugene, OCD, *I Want to See God*, Cork, 1953.

——————, *I am a Daughter of the Church*, Cork, 1955.

Maritain, Jacques, 'St. John of the Cross, Practitioner of Contemplation'; 'Todo y Nada', *The Degrees of Knowledge*, New York: Charles Scribner's Sons, 1959, pp 310-383.